FUN
IS
THERAPEUTIC

FUN
IS
THERAPEUTIC

A Recreation Book to Help
Therapeutic Recreation Leaders by People
Who Are Leading Recreation

By

ARDIS STEVENS, M.Ed.

Director of Recreation
Brattleboro Retreat
Brattleboro, Vermont

With a Foreword by

Donald F. Bridgeman, D.P.E.

Director of Undergraduate Community
and Outdoor Recreation
Springfield College, Springfield, Massachusetts

CHARLES C THOMAS · PUBLISHER
Springfield · Illinois · U.S.A.

Published and Distributed Throughout the World by
CHARLES C THOMAS • PUBLISHER
BANNERSTONE HOUSE
301-327 East Lawrence Avenue, Springfield, Illinois, U.S.A.
NATCHEZ PLANTATION HOUSE
735 North Atlantic Boulevard, Fort Lauderdale, Florida, U.S.A.

© *1972, by* CHARLES C THOMAS • PUBLISHER
ISBN 0-398-02421-9
Library of Congress Catalog Card Number: 73-187678

With THOMAS BOOKS *careful attention is given to all details of
manufacturing and design. It is the Publisher's desire to present books
that are satisfactory as to their physical qualities and artistic possibilities
and appropriate for their particular use.* THOMAS BOOKS *will be true
to those laws of quality that assure a good name and good will.*

Printed in the United States of America
I-1

Dedicated to the recreation leaders everywhere who are bringing fun to the ill, aging and handicapped and making their lives of enforced leisure a little happier.

THE WORLD IS BEAUTIFUL

The world is beautiful because . . .
    God makes the trees grow,
    Rain makes the grass grow,
    And I like to slide on ice.
The world is beautiful because . . .
    Spaghetti and meatballs make me feel good,
    Birds are fun to feed,
    And peace is a good word to say.
The world is beautiful because . . .
    People help other people out,
    And friends are fun to have.
The world is beautiful because . . .
    The sun is yellow and warm and points at you,
    Snow is good to eat,
    And God is my favorite person.
The world is beautiful because . . .
    Snow comes from heaven,
    Summer means lazy days,
    And wouldn't it be nice if everyone were good.
The world is beautiful because . . .
    God makes it so.

An original poem in free verse composed by the children in the Dramatics and Story Club, Dr. Joseph H. Ladd School, Exeter, Rhode Island.

CONTRIBUTORS

BETTY ABBOTT

Recreation Supervisor
Department of Recreation
Concord, New Hampshire

ANN ANDERSON

Activities Director
Mayflower House
Plymouth, Massachusetts

JEANNETTE BOLANDER

Recreation Therapist
Medical Center
Burlington, Vermont

HELEN BROCKLESBY

Director of Recreation
Poet's Seat Nursing Home
Greenfield, Massachusetts

TERRY BROWN

Physical Therapist Aide
Caverly Child Health Center
Pittsford, Vermont

BRUCE CAMPBELL

Director of Volunteers and Recreation
Veterans Administration Hospital
White River Junction, Vermont

MURIEL CLARK

Crafts Specialist
Bellows Falls, Vermont

Fun Is Therapeutic

ANITA COX, R.N., ADMINISTRATOR

Hillcrest Nursing Home
Fitchburg, Massachusetts

JOAN DAVIS, M.S.

Specialist in Therapeutic Recreation
Department of Parks, Recreation and Conservation
Yonkers, New York

ARCHIE DeANGELUS

Recreation and Park Director
Dalton, Massachusetts

EDITH GOULD

Activity Director
Smith Nursing Home
Millbury, Massachusetts

FLORENCE HALLOWELL

Activities Director
Convalescent and Nursing Home of Dalton
Dalton, Massachusetts

SANDRA JIROUTEK

Activities Director
Wayside Nursing Home
Worcester, Massachusetts

HARRIET JODOIN

Activities Director
Holyoke Nursing Home, Inc.
Holyoke, Massachusetts

JEANNE KAY

Director of Recreation
Cohasset Knoll Extended Care Facility
Cohasset, Massachusetts

LOUISE KEITH

Activities Director
Day Care Program, Boston State Hospital
Dorchester, Massachusetts

MARGARET MADDOCKS

Nursing Home Consultant
Vermont Department of Health
Burlington, Vermont

RAYMOND M. MAESTO

Recreational Therapist
Worcester State Hospital
Worcester, Massachusetts

MARGARET MARION

Activity Director
Hillcrest Nursing Home
Fitchburg, Massachusetts

DOREEN MORSE

Recreational Therapist
New England Medical Center Hospital
Boston, Massachusetts

JUDITH MURDOCK

Activities Director
McKerley Nursing Home
Concord, New Hampshire

GERALD O'MORROW, Ed.D.

Associate Professor of Recreation
Indiana State University
Terre Haute, Indiana

SHIRLEY SMITH

Director of Volunteers
Northampton State Hospital
Northampton, Massachusetts

ELIZABETH SMOCK

Play Teacher
Athol Memorial Hospital
Athol, Massachusetts

SPRINGFIELD COLLEGE SOCIAL RECREATION CLASS

Springfield, Massachusetts

PETER STEELE

Carrier Clinic Recreation Department
Belle Mead, New Jersey

BLANCHE STOUGHTON

Activities Director
Sullivan County Nursing Hospital
Claremont, New Hampshire

WILLIAM TOMPKINS, DIRECTOR

Trailside Museum
Forest Park
Springfield, Massachusetts

CHARLES TATRO

Director of Recreation
Brandon Training School
Brandon, Vermont

JUDITH WEST

Activity Leader
Rutland Mental Health Service, Inc.
Rutland, Vermont

FOREWORD

THE FOUR-DAY WORK week has become a reality in the work schedule of several large corporations. Educators, politicians and clergy are already voicing concern regarding how the worker will use all this new found leisure time. However, we have always had too great a percentage of our population who had to look forward to years and even a lifetime without the joy and satisfaction derived from productive work or organized programs of recreation. Our physically and mentally handicapped, along with the elderly of our country, make up these often forgotten people.

It is heartening to discover a book which has been written for the sole purpose of putting laughter and enjoyment into some of these lonely days. Ardis Stevens has a complete approach to providing programs for the elderly and handicapped. The principles and methods of testing and adapting activity are clearly defined. The professional recreational therapist or the volunteer worker will find a short curriculum of philosophy and theory for working with atypical individuals. The real treasures of the book, however, are in the encyclopedia of active and passive activities and programs.

The author recognizes that no one has been able to accurately evaluate the capacity of patients to enjoy recreational activity. She suggests that each patient participating will reap individual rewards that may defy measurement. Her own positive evaluative observations of patients enjoying recreational activity is merit enough to institute some of her programs. The broad treatment of recreational activity to include music, dramatics, crafts and games provides programs for even those persons with seriously limited physical capacity.

It is difficult to believe that there is any person who would not profit from exposure to some of these activities, if given the opportunity. Now it behooves those of us who work with these people to take this storehouse of ideas and convert them into action.

DONALD F. BRIDGEMAN

PREFACE

A BALLOON BASKETBALL GAME is in full swing at a Senior Citizens' Party when the leader notices that a participant with a history of cardiac illness is getting over-excited. She stops the game after the next point won amid shouts of protest. Upon explaining that she does not want to contribute to heart attacks, the cardiac patient replies, "But can you think of a better way to go?"

A little girl with cerebral palsy, unable to speak or to stand alone, laughs with joy as she leans against her bed and walks as she follows a big balloon that her teacher tosses from one end of the bed to the other.

A group of trainable mentally retarded teenagers dance gaily through a Virginia Reel and swing through a square dance at a party.

A severely crippled child wears a smile of pure ecstasy as he is pushed in his wheelchair around the hall with other children as they do a circle dance at a party.

A CVA patient with his left side paralyzed makes sounds of happiness as he retrieves the ball with his good right arm in a game of "Hot Potato" and passes it on to the next person.

A mute mental patient in an art class talks about gathering turkey eggs on the farm where she lived as a child, while she draws a stone wall and a tree to show where the turkeys made their nests.

A shy, withdrawn, mentally ill adult is drawn into a hilarious game of Musical Chairs, becomes the life of the party, and starts on the road to mental health.

Several elderly patients sit in a circle and sway their bodies to the strains of waltz music and clap their hands in time to marches and polkas. One lady asks if she may try standing up, and then takes some faltering steps as she waltzes for the first time in many years.

Children with various physical handicaps swim and splash as happily as normal children.

All of these people are included in the category of *ill, aging* or *handicapped.* The *therapeutic* prescription which was being used to restore or enhance good health with these people was *fun.*

The persons dispensing the medication were friendly, exuberant, warm recreation leaders who live the philosophy that *recreation is for everyone.*

There are too many people who are confined to bed, wheelchairs or walkers, residents of nursing homes or homes for the aged, patients in hospitals and institutions for the mentally ill, retarded, or physically handicapped, who are being denied the therapeutic benefit of fun. Supervisors, doctors, and nursing personnel all too frequently are heard to say that their patients are too sick or too old or too handicapped or too regressed to participate in a recreation program.

Many recreation leaders and volunteers are proving that this is untrue; that every person, unless moribund, is capable of responding in some way to *fun.*

This book includes many of the activities, programs and devices used by therapeutic recreation leaders to share with other leaders in therapeutic settings who are serving so effectively in the field, and are proving that *Fun is Therapeutic.*

ARDIS STEVENS

ACKNOWLEDGMENTS

THE AUTHOR IS INDEBTED to the many leaders in recreation who have shared their philosophy, ideas for programs and their favorite recreational activities for this book; to Don Bridgeman, whose interest in total recreation is an inspiration to his colleagues, his students and those whom he recreates; to the members of her long suffering staff who have provided fun for everyone while she was writing about it; and especially to her boss, Dr. J. Douglass Sharpe, Superintendent of Brattleboro Retreat, whose interest and support has provided opportunities for the author to conduct workshops in therapeutic recreation at the hospital and other agencies and to "get into the field" to share ideas with others.

A.S.

CONTENTS

FUN

IS

THERAPEUTIC

Chapter 1

WHAT IS THERAPEUTIC?

THERE HAS BEEN MUCH dialogue among professional recreationists, the medical profession and laymen in an effort to define *therapeutic recreation*. Webster defines *therapeutic* as *of or relating to the treatment of diseases or disorders by remedial agents or methods*. We could say then, that recreation is a *remedial agent*. Others have defined therapeutic recreation in a variety of ways.

It might clarify the issue over "what is therapeutic recreation?" if the term were "recreation in a therapeutic setting." Recreation leaders do not don any magic mantle when they go into a hospital, nursing home or other agency for the care of the ill, aging or handicapped. They use the same tools and devices for leading recreation as the leader in the community center, Senior Center, camp or playground. The only difference is that the leader in the therapeutic setting must adapt the program of recreation to accommodate those in wheelchairs, braces or walkers; the bedridden; the mentally ill or retarded; the confused or depressed or discouraged. A person does not lose his capacity for having fun when he breaks his leg, or has a heart attack, or becomes mentally ill or gets old. The mentally retarded is not without the ability to play just because he responds more slowly than others.

The recreation leader in the therapeutic setting differs from the leader in community recreation only in his understanding of the special needs of the ill, aging and handicapped. He has a knowledge of the medical needs of those whom he recreates. He knows how to involve his patients in *normal* recreation activities by modification. He has compassion, but not pity; a positive approach, never saying "they cannot have fun because they are too sick"; he has a firm faith in the philosophy that "recreation is for everyone." He enjoys fun and has the ability to involve others in having fun, also.

Leaders in recreation have different ways of defining *therapeutic recreation.*

Therapeutic recreation is the intervention in the physical, emotion and/or social behaviour of the individual to bring about the further growth and development of the individual and is in accord with the mission of the agency providing the service.

Therapeutic recreation is any recreational activity in which patients and a recreational therapist engage for the purpose of diagnostic evaluation with the therapeutic goal of assisting the patients in their physical, mental and social adjustments and rehabilitation.

Therapeutic recreation is the physical and mental help given a person participating in some form of recreation.

Therapeutic recreation is that which is curative. The therapeutic recreation leader applies a remedy (fun) to cure the diseases of idleness, loneliness, boredom, fatigue, depression and fear. Happiness is a positive emotion. Happiness can be a vital part of medical and psychological progress.

Therapeutic recreation is a program to keep people mentally alert even though they are physically handicapped and to keep them feeling useful and happy.

Therapeutic recreation is using the talents and abilities of patients involved in an activity, active or passive, to help them fulfill their need to love and live their life to the fullest.

Therapeutic recreation is a human service based on the philosophy that each man is responsible for meeting his own needs and each man has a need for recreative experience. It is the responsibility of the therapeutic recreator to aid people in overcoming the limitations (physical, psychological, intellectual, social, economic, chronological, informational) that defer him in his efforts to meet this need.

All recreation is therapeutic! By the very nature of its rewards of satisfaction and enjoyment recreation generates an inner well-being which aids in the process of rehabilitation and good health.

Therapeutic recreation is when the director says to the

group, "your ideas are great; let us plan, create, relax and enjoy them."

Recreation within the hospital is the same as recreation in the community. Recreation is recreation is recreation. The only differences are found in the clientele. Recreation in the community, as recreation in the hospital, must be based on the needs of the people. As people are different, so are activities. Recreation remains recreation, not therapy.

Recreation is a diversional activity *voluntarily chosen* by the patient for sheer enjoyment and stimulation. Recreation is not meant to be a cure for patients or to rehabilitate them. However, when patients adopt a healthy attitude toward physical disabilities and become involved in individual and group endeavors, improvement in their physical and mental conditions become a natural and anticipated by-product of recreation. Recreation is a basic human need and a part of normal living. For patients in nursing homes, recreational activities are as essential as food, shelter and nursing care. Some patients in nursing homes have arrived there rather precipitously and they anticipate remaining there for a long time. They are often afraid, insecure and lonely. They feel cast out from the family and familiar life into a strange, confined and often hostile world filled with routine, boredom and fears. To assist them in adjusting to this difficult situation, a recreation program is essential.

First of all, patients need to relax and enjoy themselves in spite of their illness and infirmities. When busy with activities, they temporarily forget their troubles and problems. Secondly, they need to find a purpose for living in their present environment and a way of contributing to life so that it will be worthwhile for themselves and for others. Thirdly, they need to socialize with and to be accepted by other patients in the home as well as by those caring for them. Finally, they occasionally need time to be alone, not time for brooding, melancholy or withdrawal, but time for reflection, meditation and spiritual refreshments. A well-rounded recreation program can help them accomplish these goals.

Living and working in Vermont is therapeutic in itself with its endowment of nature to stimulate the most tired mind and afflicted body. At Caverly, its sophical school master once a day closes the math books, picks up his guitar and stirs his pupils into song. Ambulatory children gather from all parts of the infirmary to hear and sing songs that never grow old. Imagine yourself a boy, anxious to run, jump and play, lying horizontally in bed for two years. Wouldn't songs like "Casey Jones," "Carolina in the Morning," "Faith, Hope and Charity" and "Down by the Riverside" carry you into a wonderful world beyond recovery.

Then there are other therapies: a brain damaged ataxic child who through skiing (which indirectly is the needed eye-foot coordination) has learned to walk again. His face reveals to you his happiness and fulfillment.

Building a snowman on a sunlit February day helps our speechless withdrawn little friend to build "Frosty's" round fat body, his eyes, nose, mouth, then attempt to speak each part.

Children are originators of creativity and the therapy room is often overflowing with little inventors. These children are masters at "make do, make shift and make over," as they develop their fine motor skills, dressing all the teddy bears and cavorting them to the music of "Teddy Bear's Picnic," each adapting his own motion most original and ideal for him.

This is only a brief portrait of Caverly's Gate to Health but I believe proof positive that the sterile white clinic table is not always the background for healing.

No matter how therapeutic recreation is defined, it is generally agreed that it is effective. Leaders of recreation in therapeutic settings have seen amazing changes in patients who have the opportunity to participate in recreation programs. In settings where a great amount of attention is given to the patient's illness, recreation programs concentrate on the patient's wellness.

Recreation is fun, and *fun is therapeutic.*

Chapter 2

WHO IS THE LEADER?

Recreation leaders come in assorted abilities. They have varied education for their jobs, and their salaries range all the way from volunteers to professionals. There are never enough leaders to supply the need, and the situation will not improve, according to statistics.

The value of a recreation leader on the staff in the therapeutic setting is becoming increasingly evident to administrators.

It has been said that "five percent of people are creative leaders; five percent are good imitators; ninety percent are followers."

There are many followers who can become creative leaders, given the opportunity and desire to acquire leadership skills.

Some of the essential qualities for creative leaders are as follows:

1. Friendliness.
2. Ability to get along with people.
3. Cheerfulness.
4. Self-confidence.
5. Persistence and patience.
6. Personality.
7. Common sense.
8. Forcefulness.
9. Dependability.
10. Social sensitivity.
11. Appearance.
12. Recreation skills.
13. Imagination.
14. Initiative.
15. A sense of humor.
16. Tact.
17. Ability to teach, and to involve others in an activity.

The recreation leader must remember that people usually do not have to participate in a recreation program. It is usually a matter of free choice. People who are ill need more encouragement than well people to participate in recreation. The job of the leader is to assess the readiness and abilities of the participant and to choose a variety of activities with suitable levels of skills and interest.

The participants should get a feeling of success and self-confidence from the activity, and above all, they should have a good time.

The following are some goals for the leader in the therapeutic setting:

1. To encourage more interaction and closer interpersonal relationships with fellow patients.
2. To provide a nonthreatening, nondemanding environment.
3. To channel hostilities into strenuous activities.
4. To overcome apprehensiveness regarding contact with people.
5. To develop a feeling of self-acceptance and importance.
6. To help the patients to relax with activities of no rigid limit or goals recommended.
7. To help the patient avoid meaningless and insoluble problems in which he becomes lost.
8. To help the patient restore his self-confidence and to enhance a feeling of worth.
9. To help the patient to assume responsibility and to face reality.
10. To provide for achievement of self-satisfaction through creative accomplishments.
11. To encourage mute and catatonic patients to speak.
12. To minimize withdrawal tendencies.
13. To orient the patient outward toward community life.
14. To provide outlets for physical tension with competitive experiences.
15. To encourage socially acceptable behaviour.
16. To provide a setting for observation and diagnostic purposes.
17. To afford personal enjoyment and satisfaction.
18. To offset empty hours, monotony and boredom.
19. To develop skills, talents and abilities.
20. To renew and refresh physical strength.
21. To enrich attitudes, interests and experiences.
22. To enable participants to explore vocational and cultural pursuits.

23. To encourage creative, inventive and expressional efforts.

Short range goals are fun, the creation of interest and a feeling of achievement.

Long range goals include the development of recreational skills, social behaviour, confidence in a group, improved habits of dress and manners and the development of leadership within a group.

The good leader shows concern for the disabilities of the participants and adapts the program to their skills.

The good leader has confidence in himself. An attitude of assurance will influence group participation.

The good leader enjoys the activity that he is leading, and his enthusiasm will rub off on the participants.

The good leader is not afraid to make mistakes but profits by them and corrects them.

The good leader *never* says that a game will not work until he has tried it. He *never* assumes that the people are too ill or too old or too retarded to participate in some form of recreation.

RECREATION KITS

Recreation kits, sometimes called "pleasure chests," are a necessary part of the recreation leaders' bag of tricks. Every leader should have a collection of recreation tools which can be carried from place to place or ward to ward. This may be an old suitcase, a wooden box with a handle or an elaborate game box constructed for the purpose. It should include hand puppets, balloons, jar rubbers, a soda bottle, scissors, a ball of heavy string, masking tape, chalk, crayons, pencils, paper, bean bags, a large inflatable rubber ball, sponges, small rubber ball, silk scarves, dowels a foot or so long, small puzzles, some lengths of clothesline, coloring books, straight and safety pins, small clothespins, crepe paper streamers, two sets of alphabet cards with large letters, dominoes, checkers, marbles, deck of cards, dice, a book of quizzes, and any other articles that might be useful in a game.

The recreation leader should make himself known in the community. He can use the radio and newspapers, and he can be available to speak at clubs and other meetings. People are usually eager to help but first they must be made aware of how and where they can help.

If there is a special program being planned, call the local news media and let them publicize the affair.

Talk to everyone and exchange ideas. Visit other agencies and see what other leaders are doing for recreation programs.

One business in our town has a wishing well. A recreation leader asked what the money was used for. The owner thought a minute and said that the recreation leader could have it if she could figure out a way to fish out the coins. Two small children went wading the next day for the coins and a front page story appeared in two newspapers. The children in pediatrics got some new playthings and the businessman got some appreciated publicity.

VOLUNTEERS

Volunteers can be of invaluable service to a recreation program. Many talented and creative people would become volunteers if they knew that they were wanted or needed.

There should, first of all, be a felt need for the services of volunteers. Secondly, this need should be communicated to potential volunteers. And finally, the volunteers should be oriented to the agency and given guidance and support.

Organizing and Maintaining a Volunteer Service Program

1. Sell your proposed programs to "Number One," who is your hospital superintendent, home director, or administrator.
2. Ask for a meeting of all chiefs of staff, department heads, or supervisors.
3. Ask each person present at the meeting whether they can use volunteers in their departments and if so, how many, how often, doing what duties and for how long each week.
4. List each duty outlined above, giving details of type of work and requirements.
5. Now that you have your demand for volunteers you must obtain your supply. When you get your program

functioning you will hopefully establish a balance between supply and demand.

6. Your next job is to sell your program to prospective
volunteers. Write up your needs and make a good story
of it. Send it or take it to the newspapers, radio and television outlets. In your story also offer your services as
speaker at any meeting of interested people.

7. Go out and recruit. Talk on the radio. If you are unable
to reach all stations have a tape cut giving your story
and needs and send this to the news outlets. Talk at
meetings of organizations; ask for volunteers; get names
and set up an interview for each.

8. When your prospective volunteers come to you, be
ready to sell your program to them. Tell them they are
needed. Show them on your tour of your establishment
where they can work.

9. Get information on all volunteer prospects: age, distance from home, choice of job as a volunteer. Try to
determine if prospects are stable. After they have started, it is very difficult to fire someone who is working
without pay.

10. Fit your volunteer list to your job list as best as possible.
Match-ups will be helped by previous screening of
volunteers. Tell your volunteers that if they are dissatis-
fied with their jobs not to quit, but rather to come back
to you for a new assignment, and keep coming back
until they find their spot.

11. Once you get your program operating, do not sit pat
on it. Get another story in the paper and on the air
relating your now functioning volunteer program and
the need for expansion.

12. Keep reminding your volunteers that you want to know
anything, good or bad, that happens to them while they
are on duty.

13. Remember the story of the two-way swinging doors at
the entrance of the hospital. Leave your problems and
woes outside them when you enter as a volunteer and
leave what you see and hear inside the doors.

14. No matter what your volunteers may say, they do appreciate some sort of thanks or certificates of appreciation. One year after your volunteer program has been going, or any time you think the program needs a lift, hold an *awards ceremony*. Make up certificates of appreciation signed by your director or administrator. Get some pictures in the paper if possible. Have pictures, names, awards and highlights published in all the local papers.

15. Strive to show no favoritism. If you allow this to happen it may destroy your program.

16. If a volunteer goes sour and needs reprimanding, do it in private. Everyone deserves this courtesy.

17. As you are expected to show no favoritism, you must also explain to your volunteers that they should not center their visits around one or two patients. We all form favorites but impress upon your volunteers that *all* patients need their attention.

18. Be honest with your volunteers and expect them to be honest with you.

19. When you turn a volunteer over to a service to work, that volunteer's training becomes the responsibility of that service. However, the volunteer is still your responsibility.

20. Finally, you will have problems that are not outlined here. When problems arise, talk them over with someone you respect. Don't be ashamed to ask for help.

The role of the volunteer has two important parts: his or her relationship with the community, and with the hospital or other agency. Through the volunteer, the community will receive its best education in relation to illness. The volunteer informs the public of the work that is being done at the agency.

Guideposts may not have been established for every situation which may arise. In this event, the volunteer should consult the head of the department under which he is serving or the director of volunteer services.

Volunteer Services' Needs

Resocialization is the key word in hospitals today, and volunteers are needed as a necessary part of the team. The needs that volunteers may fill are many and varied. Doing something with the patients is the easiest way to establish a friendship, and helps to break up their daily routine.

Volunteers should be assigned to the same hall each time they visit so that good relationships can be established, and so that the residents will be able to look forward to regular visits from their volunteers. Regular volunteers enjoy developing their own programs within the framework of hospital rules, as they become better acquainted with the ladies or men on the hall to which they are assigned.

Specific requests may be made by departments at times. Other programs may be built around a specific talent or interest of a volunteer.

Volunteers are recruited in many ways. One good way is to talk to church and community organizations. Volunteers are helpful visitors, party planners and life savers when the recreation director needs someone to help with transporting patients to appointments.

Volunteers are used as assistants at arts and crafts, helping with parties, and planning and helping with religious meetings. Candy stripers are also used.

Volunteers are recruited through local high schools and Girl Scouts. They assist with parties, programs and decorations.

Recruit by word of mouth and use volunteers as friendly visitors; for giving patients manicures, coffee socials, and birthday parties; for making ceramics and tray favors; and at sing-a-longs.

Volunteers were recruited through the volunteer service of the hospital. They were filtered into recreation work through interviews with the director of voluntary service and the director of recreation. The volunteers were used during the day for bringing flowers, newspapers or the hospital gift cart around to the patients, or simply as conversational stimulators. In the evenings, volunteers showed movies, hosted speaker and guest entertainers, and helped in stimulating and encouraging patients to attend functions. Some volunteers initiated and planned their own programs such as bingo or game nights.

Daughters of patients furnished musical entertainment, did baking for special events, brought a sewing machine once a week to help with quilt-making, and helped serve at coffee socials.

Home auxiliary conducts Wednesday evening Whist parties. The Gospel Singers conduct "Hymnspiration" song times. The volunteers also help with bingo, crafts, birthday parties, holidays or give a one man show of various talents. Volunteers also provide transportation for patients.

Volunteers help with arts and crafts, assist in demonstrations, organization of rock collections, discussion groups, and bingo. They also help with decorations for parties on holidays, entertainment for monthly birthday parties and sing-a-longs.

Volunteers are used on buses, with swimming and other activities and receive a great deal of satisfaction in their jobs.

Chapter 3

WHAT CAN WE DO TODAY?

THE QUESTION MOST often asked by recreation leaders in therapeutic agencies where they have the same clients for programs over long periods of time is "what can we do for recreation today?"

For the inexperienced leader, this is a real and agonizing problem. In addition to a lack of experience, there may be other problems like inadequate space, few recreation tools, shortage of help, and difficulty in motivating patients or clients.

One solution to the question is workshops in recreation leadership. The recreation leader should take advantage of every opportunity to learn skills and to share ideas with others.

Another is to read everything available on the subject of recreation, especially books on games, and adapt ideas to the individual situation.

Use imagination and innovation to develop exciting recreation programs.

Some points to consider in planning a recreation program are as follows:

1. What are the abilities and interests of the people for whom you are planning recreation?
2. Where can you conduct your programs? Is there available space?
3. What do you have for recreation tools such as record players, slide and movie projectors, sports equipment, and equipment for games and crafts?
4. Plan a program full of interest, information, inspiration, instruction and innovations.
5. Plan ahead. Make a weekly or monthly calendar of events.
6. Plan worthwhile activities which will appeal to the needs and interests of the participants.

7. Involve the people who will participate in the recreation program in the planning of it. A Patients' Recreation Committee is invaluable.
8. Build your program around religious and secular holidays.
9. What can you, the leader, do best? Is it music, games, crafts, sports or what?
10. Think positively. "Cannot" or "will not" are not part of a recreation leader's vocabulary.

A well-balanced recreation program consists of creative activities: music, drama, arts and crafts; physical activities: games, dancing, exercises; mental activities: puzzles, quizzes, brain teasers, study groups, learning "how to"; social activities: parties, dances, picnics, trips; and service activities: fund-raising, stuffing envelopes for organizations, bandage rolling, and other helping practices.

PROGRAM SUGGESTIONS

Several ideas for programs have been contributed by recreation leaders and they are as follows:

All residents enjoy the weekly short subject movies. Ambulatory residents enjoy shopping trips and short outings.

Some programs our residents like are the ecumenical church services, folk masses (bringing the new to the old), the annual picnic, and the Christmas Party with Santa.

Entertainment using dancing classes and kindergarten groups are popular. Residents also entered a float in the Civic Day Parade and received third prize.

My patients love to sing and we have old fashioned hymn sings. The old hymns and the spirituals are their favorites.

We had a Spring Fashion Show with all men models who modeled women's clothes, which was enjoyed by all. The therapeutic value of this show was the laughter.

We held an auction using play money, each bill representing one dollar, with each resident having twenty-five dollars. We auctioned homemade cookies, fruit, jewelry, cigars and cigarettes. They really yelled and screamed on this one.

Use "What is it?" ads from *Yankee* magazine as a guessing

game or contest. If one writes to Savogran, Norwood, Massachusetts, they will supply a variety of past ads free. This activity is particularly appealing and useful with people who are aged.

Of all the programs I have used, possibly the Christmas Party which was arranged in cooperation with the nursing staff and prepared for the patients was most appreciated. Refreshments, invitations, enthusiasm and decorations were prepared by the staff. During the party, cranberry chains were made by the patients to decorate the tree which was placed in the hall.

Sewing bees are held each Tuesday morning. A patient's daughter brings her sewing machine and while the ladies sew personal clothes of patients and replace buttons, she stitches basted squares for lap robes which the ladies have worked on the week before. We make them for folks who have to sit most of the time and they add a cheery and colorful note. The personal sewing makes the women feel at home, and it is a great service to the patients who have mending to be done. It is a good time for the ladies to have a gab fest, too.

Bandage rolling is a very important activity because many folks have done this important service in their churches in the past. Using old sheets, I measure every two inches and slit them. One person strips, another prepares them over her hands and places them in a bag or box. Then Wednesday afternoons everyone meets in our main room and rolls them into bandages and ties them. Very good for visiting and the work makes them feel needed by the community. The Red Cross takes the bandages. This is a good community service!

A coffee social is a time for fun. I put records on our stereo (newly purchased from recreational funds), and a volunteer helps serve coffee and donut holes. Diabetics get their own treats of cookies or crackers. We sing the old songs, visit, tell stories and jokes. This is a very happy morning get-together and is eagerly awaited each week. This is a once a week affair purposely to keep it a treat for both men and women. It is almost like a morning out.

Reading sessions are fun. The patients choose a book to their liking and we gather together in a room where it is quiet and I read aloud. We all enjoy this very much and discuss the story or our own personal experiences that come to mind as the story brings back memories.

I find that gathering around a piano for singing is very successful.

I have used patients' variety shows, dances, exercises for females, and sing-a-longs as special programs.

Swimming, water volleyball, bowling, funnel ball, Junior Olympics, snow races, basketball and special playground activities have been used for mentally retarded children.

I find simple card games like Fish, Rummy and Pitch, checkers, and group entertainment are most successful. We have speakers come in and talk on many subjects. Some of the volunteers have brought in slide shows of trips which they have taken. One of our most successful ventures was not an activity but a thing, which led to many peaceful and rewarding hours for those patients who could do very little active recreating. This was a 30 gallon fish aquarium set out in the hall. Some patients enjoyed just sitting and watching the fish and learning about them from books. An activity which was a big success but a lot of work was painting the patients' television room. The patients in wheelchairs used long-handled brushes or rollers with paint pans easily accessible on the floor. "Paint Day" was extended to two days because of unexpected problems with thin paint and a dark undercolor. All was done by patients except the trim near the ceiling which was done by a therapist. Wheelchairs and floor were covered with a plastic sheeting.

We had a very successful Christmas Fair and sold patients' handicraft, white elephants, and Christmas cookies baked and decorated by patients in supervised groups.

We encourage all of our residents to get dressed daily and we try to help them lead as near a normal life as possible. Our recreation department has become active in planning tours, shopping sprees, and outside visits for our family. In many cases the elderly mind is alert despite a failing body. We feel that all of our residents must be treated with respect and dignity. We try to keep them busy and happy.

Our Arts and Crafts Department makes stuffed toys for distribution to worthwhile organizations such as orphanages and hospitals. At Christmas they sent some packages to a Korean orphanage. A group of residents has done work for the post office preparing Christmas mailing kits, and they have worked for the March of Dimes. It may be an old cliché but everyone needs to be needed.

Our most recent fun has been making tapes to be played to patients or employees who have had to go to the general hospital and miss the familiar voices.

A Christmas Party was held in the morning, followed by a cocktail hour and a Christmas buffet set up on a shuffleboard table covered with a sheet of plywood.

An Interest Index is sometimes helpful in planning recreation programs. Have the participants in recreation programs indicate the activities which they enjoy or would like to learn to enjoy.

Weekly or monthly calendars may be printed on construction paper or on calendars made especially for the purpose. These can be displayed on bulletin boards or other public spots.

Chapter 4

FUN WITH PARTIES

Parties are fun and should be a regular feature of all recreation programs. All holidays are excuses for having a party and there is an endless number of party themes around which to build parties.

Every party needs the following:

1. Invitations. Even in an agency or institution where people are living, each should get a personal invitation to a party. Make invitations for each person if possible. Colorful posters for bulletin boards help to spread the word. Do both, and talk it up.

2. Decorations. They may be simple or elaborate, but they are a must for setting the party mood. The patients or residents may spend many preparty hours preparing decorations. Appropriate cutouts from construction paper can be taped to the walls with masking tape. Be sure that each person has his name on his "creation."

   Tip on taping: Try a tiny bit in an obscure spot on the wall to determine if the paint will come off with the tape when the decoration is removed. Masking tape is more effective than other tapes and is less likely to remove paint. Roll a piece of tape into a little circle, sticky-side out, and put it on the back of whatever is being taped to the wall, woodwork, furniture or windows. The tape will not show and it makes a much better looking decoration.

3. Costumes. Use costumes whenever possible. Even a funny hat or a colorful scarf will add to the party atmosphere. Save things like these for parties.

4. Themes. Invitations, decorations, costumes, games and refreshments can all be built around a theme.

International Party

This theme party is suitable for October to recognize United Nations Day. Card tables are placed around the room to represent cafe style. A red, white and blue color scheme is used in the table settings and decorations. White cloths can be used with either red or blue streamers crisscrossing the table top. Simple centerpieces to set the table off may be marshmallows with toothpick replicas of flags of various nations. Let the residents make the centerpieces. The patients are asked to bring some object from their rooms to represent a country. They may prove to be quite creative. One woman brought a basket of flowers that had been a tray favor on May Day but on this day they were alpine flowers from the Swiss Alps. Another lady brought a Christmas elf which had been a decoration on a shelf. For this occasion, the elf became a leprachaun from Ireland. One man did not have anything to bring so he stood up and spoke a phrase in French. Some patients do have objects from foreign countries in their rooms. The object of this program is to involve the patient. Each one was asked to display the object which he had brought and to say a few words about it.

Refreshments may be Chinese fortune cookies and a punch with a special name, like Jamaica Rum. If fortune cookies are served, each patient may take a turn reading his fortune.

Punch recipe: Fill a tall glass one half to three quarters full of unsweetened grapefruit juice over ice. Fill the remainder with diet ginger ale. Add a teaspoon of rum flavoring and mint. Serve with brightly colored straws.

Circus Daze

This is a Carnival-type Progressive Party which includes invitations which can be a clown holding a handful of balloons. Each balloon has printed on it the time, place, date and other information about the party. Or cut an envelope so that it resembles a cage with gratings. A paper animal inside has party information written on him.

There are six or more booths, each with a different color. You can also have the booths represent a circus animal.

Refreshments can be popcorn and pink lemonade.

As each person enters the room he receives a small clown's hat upon which are six colored buttons. The top button is used for a "Musical Mixer." All with red buttons at the top get together and sing a song like "Yankee Doodle Dandy." Blues will sing "Old Black Joe" and so on. At the sound of a signal, each person moves to the booth of the color of his second button. Various games are played at each booth. After an interval of play, the gong sounds again and everyone moves to the booth of the third color on his hat. Keep the crowd moving until all have played the game at each booth. Prizes may be given to the winners at each booth. End the party with a Circus Parade to the refreshment booth.

Westward Ho Party

Invitations may be in the shape of a Texas hat, with information around the brim. They could also be a stagecoach or an Indian tepee. Use your imagination. Decorations can be western hats, covered wagons, cowboy boots, lariats, tablecloths decorated with "brands" or anything with a Western flavor. Refreshments can be cowboy punch and golden nuggets (cookies). Give each person an envelope with a cattle brand on the front and sealed orders inside. The person goes to the game with the same brand. After playing that game a few minutes, all move to another game. Odd brand numbers go to the right, and even brand numbers move to the left. This gets the players different partners with whom to play games.

Some game suggestions on which the leader might improvise: Sutter's Mill (Penny Drop); Devil's Gorge (Milk Bottle Lift); Deadman's Ravine (Pingpong Trial); Ambush Rock (Candle Shoot).

Black Cat Party

Write invitations on a cutout black cat with white ink, or on yellow cats with black ink. Use Halloween decorations, with all sorts of cats. This is a passive party. Refreshments can be cider and doughnuts or catnip tea and cookies.

Lucky Cat Mixer: Give each person a small paper cat as he enters the room. One cat is marked for the "lucky cat." Players move around the room shaking hands and exchanging cats. On the signal to stop, the person with the lucky cat wins a prize.

This is a Cat: Players sit in a circle. The leader passes a paper cat to the person on his right and says "This is a cat." That person says to the first person "A what" and the first person replies "A cat." Number 2 then passes the cat to Number 3 saying "This is a cat." Number 3 says to Number 2 "A What?" and Number 2 says to Number 1 "A What?" The first person replies to Number 2 "A cat" who turns to Number 3 and says "A cat." Keep passing the cat around the circle with this dialogue. The "A what?" must be repeated by each person back to Number 1 and then "A cat" passed back to the person who has received the cat. The group should be divided into two teams and the game used as relay. The team who can pass the cat to the end of the line first wins.

Cats Galore: Give each person pencil and paper and let everyone see how many words they can write down including the word "cat" in a certain length of time. Words such as cattle, catastrophe, catatonic and catalog would be included. Give a prize to the person who gets the most.

End the party with the singing of the Black Cat Society anthem "Three Blind Mice."

Football Party

Preparty activities could include making invitations in the shape of a football for each person. Posters, announcements and other advertising before the party should be done. Decorations may be flags, crepe paper, football cutouts and other autumn decorations.

At the beginning of the party, designate players for two teams and let them choose a team name. Others can be the band with majorettes, referees, water boys, cheerleaders and other officials. Give the football team players some paper bags from which to make helmets, and old jerseys padded with newspapers for uniforms.

The band, with bells, tonettes, pan lids, and any other noise making equipment can lead the Homecoming parade followed by the cheerleaders, team members and spectators. Persons in wheelchairs may join the parade which can proceed through the institution where noise will not be too upsetting.

"First Quarter Play" may include a Football Throwing Conest. Blow up paper bags and tie with a string. Have a player from each team stand on the throwing line and throw the football as far as possible. The player who throws it the farthest gets a point for his team. Let every team member try.

"Second Quarter Play" could be the time for the game Six-Yard Scrimmage. Line up three members from each team in a straight line:

x x x o o o

1 2 3 4 5 6

The leader throws large dice on the floor, or the players may throw their own. Number 1 may throw a 6 and Number 2 throw a 2. If players are ambulatory, set up six chairs in six rows. Or draw squares on the floor with chalk. If players are in wheelchairs, a chart may be used with markers for each player. Each player moves back the number of squares which he throws on the dice. The first person to reach the "six-yard line" wins. Or the team to get all of their players to the "six-yard line" first wins.

Half-time entertainment could be celebrated by each team having its cheerleaders lead an original cheer and a peppy song. The teams could also do quick skits for the entertainment program.

A Football Pass Relay could be in the "Third Quarter." Teams are lined up in two lines facing. The captain for each team stands in front of his team. At the signal, each captain tosses a football to the first player on his team, who passes it back. The captain then tosses it to the next player in line and so on to the end. The first player in line may become the new captain to repeat the action until all players have been the captain. The team who finishes this action first wins the game.

"Fourth Quarter Play" could be the game Football Touchdown. Use any quiz or mental game with the team giving the correct answer to each question first a point for his team. The team with the most points at the end of the game wins.

At the end of the fourth quarter, determine which team has

won the most points for the whole football game, and celebrate with a Victory Dance. Have everyone join in a Snake Dance, Hokey Pokey and other dances. Those in wheelchairs may participate.

Snowflake Frolic

Decorate the room with snowflakes made by the residents and suspended from the ceiling with yarn or string. Snowflakes may be made with paper doilies cut into various shapes and decorated with Magic Markers.

Indoor Winter Carnival: Use the decorations from the Snowflake Frolic and add flags, crepe paper streamers and ski posters.

Snow Sculpturing Contest

Give everyone a piece of white paper, newspaper, paper napkins or towels and have them tear a sculpture from it with their hands. Some may need help with tearing. Tape the finished sculpture up on the walls and have a panel of judges award ribbons.

Carnival Torch Relay

Make a "torch" out of rolled construction paper, a dowel, baton or newspaper. Divide the players into teams. If they are in a circle around the room, designate the dividing line between the teams. Give a torch to the first person on each team. At the signal, the torch is passed from one player to the next until it reaches the last person on the team. The first team to "pass the torch" to the end of the line wins.

Snowball Throwing Contest

Use styrofoam balls. As players are seated in a circle or whatever formation they happen to be in, let two people compete by throwing the snowballs as far as possible. The person who throws the greatest distance wins. The players can be divided into teams and the combined scores kept to determine which team wins.

Snowshoe Race

Divide players into teams. Give the first person on each team a badminton racket or cardboard "snowshoe." On the signal, the first person passes the snowshoe to the next player on the right. The first team to get the snowshoe to the end of the line wins.

If the players are ambulatory, give each player two pieces of cardboard and line up at the "starting gate." On the signal, each player throws down a piece of cardboard and steps on it while he places the other piece inches in front of his feet. He then steps on that one and picks up the one behind and throws that one down ahead. The first player to reach the finish line wins the race. Do not let players slide along the floor on their snowshoes. They must be picked up and put down before stepping on them.

Snowman Bowl

Use a portable plastic bowling set which can be obtained in any toy department or with trading stamps. If one is not available, use plastic detergent bottles and a whiffle ball. With a Magic Marker, transform the bowling pins into snowmen with big eyes and a bow tie. Players may be seated in a circle, and the pins set up a few feet in front of each bowler as it becomes his turn. Give each player in turn the bowling ball (snowball) and in three tries, see how many snowmen each can bowl over. Keep score and give a small prize to the winner.

Refreshments may be marshmallows dipped in frosting and rolled in shredded coconut to make snowballs. Serve with punch or hot cocoa. If the party is for younger folks, popcorn balls could be served.

Some other party themes to use for "imagination joggers":

Latin America Fiesta	Old Year Party
Around the World Party	Turkey Shoot
Mexican Fiesta	Easter Bonnet Parade
Space Party	Wild West Rodeo
Yule Do	Back at the Ranch Party
Affair of the Heart	Old Timers Ball
Kiddie Kaper	Shamrock Shindig

Bunny Hop (for Easter)   May Daze Party
Graduates Party   School Daze Party
Firecracker Frolic   Beach Party

Use your imagination; change names to fit the party theme; use costumes made of towels, scarves, crepe paper, old clothes or anything.

The following are some rules for a good party:

1. Make it fun for everyone from the moment he arrives.
2. Keep the party moving: "Stagnation breeds defeat."
3. Give directions clearly, briefly and in a manner so that all participants can hear, then get on with the playing.
4. Plan activities to "absorb" people as they enter the room for the party.
5. *Know* what you are going to do; *know* the games that you will lead; have all the props and equipment ready; and be prepared to change your whole program at a minute's notice.

Chapter 5

FUN WITH MUSIC

RESPONSE TO MUSIC seems to be an automatic reflex. The blind can hear it, the deaf can feel it, the most withdrawn respond with a tap of the toe or finger, the most uncommunicative sing the old familiar songs with a record, and the child moves in rhythm to the music. Watch the mood change as a crowd responds to an approaching parade band; observe the wheelchair patient as a polka, march or waltz is played; notice the drift of people toward the piano where a volunteer is belting out old songs; marvel at the deaf child as he feels the beat of square dance music through the floor and dances the figure in perfect rhythm; listen to the senile, bedridden patient whisper the words along with the playing of a familiar hymn; swallow the lump in your throat that you get when you watch the tears stream down the cheeks of a catatonic patient as she listens to Mitch Miller's record of "Love's Old Sweet Song." Tune in to the response around you and see if you can honestly say "There are some patients who cannot be reached with ANY activity."

You need not be a skilled musician to provide fun with music. Set up a record player and put on some records. Use imagination and devise your own methods of getting the ill, handicapped and aging to respond to musical activities.

Clap-out Rhythms

Clap out the rhythm of familiar songs without the music and let the group guess what tune it is. The players may be divided into two teams. Let one clap out a song like "Jingle Bells" and the other team tries to guess it. Then the other team might tap out "Goodnight Ladies."

Follow the Leader

The leader, with music from a record player or piano, does various motions to the rhythm. All of the people in the room do the same motion. When the leader changes the motion, all follow. The leader might start by clapping hands, then change to stamping feet, then to swaying the body from side to side. Ask different people in the room to be the leader. This can be good exercise as well as fun. Always use peppy music.

Band Concert

Ask each person in the room to choose a band instrument which he is going to pretend to play. Give some suggestions, or even designate someone to play the bass fiddle, trombone or to be the conductor. Put a march record or other lively tune on the record player and everyone "plays" along with the music. Give several people turns at being the conductor.

Rhythm Band

Get a collection of noise makers for a rhythm band or kitchen band. Sticks to hit together, blocks with sandpaper glued on one side to rub together, tamborines, tin can drums, tonettes, bells, pan covers, old washboards, spoons, or anything else that makes noise can be used. A rhythm band can be as simple or as sophisticated as one wants to make it. The important thing is to have lively music as accompaniment for the band. The band members may sit down to play, or lie in bed, or march around the room, or all three if you have room and a mixed group of people.

DANCE THERAPY

Dance therapy is the planned use of any aspects of dance to aid in the physical and psychic integration of the individual. Start at the point where the patient is. If he is depressed, start with a circle formation with music that is slow, and use slow stretches. Start with both hands behind the back, and bring forth one finger at a time. After stretching and showing it, return it to the position behind the back until all of the fingers on one hand have been used, then do the other hand. Stretch up and out each time. Then work on circles with the wrists, elbows and shoulders; swings and circles with the arms; rotation of the head; bending side to side; bending upper torso over and sitting up straight; slouching and sitting up straight; lifting hips one at a time; raising knees and legs and feet; and making circles with the feet. Then stand up and bend and reach up tall and sway side to side.

Change the music to something more spirited like a polka or contemporary music. With one hand and then the other, travel up arms and around bodies, feeling the "wholeness" of the body. Then "wash up" for the dance. Using hands, wash the face, neck, ears, shoulders, on down to the toes. Shake off excess water and dry with a towel. Wiggle with the drying movement. This activity helps with concentration outside the body and a feeling of the self as a whole moving in a group.

After everyone has prepared for the dance, all move into a circle with hands joined and continue motions to music.

With a hyperactive patient, use music to work off the hyperactivity. Polkas, marches, highly rhythmic types of music help them to express that energy constructively through basic movements. Work down to a slower, more relaxing tempo with swings and creative expression.

One has to be sensitive to the needs of the group and work accordingly. Whatever the patient has to offer in movements is used and sometimes to that person's surprise. When a patient is asked "What do you have to offer the group?" the answer is usually "I don't know" with a shaking of the head. Take the shaking of the head and add it to other movements. Or no question may be asked. Just pick up motions from persons in the group.

Scarf Dance

Women enjoy this more than men. Give each person in the group a scarf or length of chiffon or anything colorful and filmy. Let each person express herself to the music as she waves her scarf.

Bean Bag Toss

Use slow to moderately fast music, depending on what you want to happen. Say the name of the person to whom you are going to toss the bean bag before the bean bag is tossed so that people will become better acquainted and interaction becomes easier. Much laughing and "freeing up" happens, plus more people are included, particularly those who are sitting on the sidelines watching.

Folk Dancing

Just because a person is handicapped is no reason for not enjoying folk dancing. Have you seen a resident of a nursing home dancing a Virginia Reel in a wheelchair or with a walker or with a cane? Have you held the hands of a bedridden or wheelchair patient and swayed to the rhythm of a waltz, or a polka or La Raspa or the Charlestown? Most dances can be adapted to include everyone.

Probably the best dance for use with all ages and capabilities is the *Hokey Pokey*. The record is available in most music stores, but if you do not have it, let everyone sing it while you do the motions.

> You put your right foot in, you take your right foot out,
> You put your right foot in and you shake it all about,
> Then you do the Hokey Pokey and you turn yourself about.
> That's what it's all about. (Wiggle and clap hands on last line.)

Continue with left foot, right hand, left hand, right elbow, left elbow, right hip, left hip, head, whole self.

Rig-a-Jig-Jig: Use the record, all sing, or have someone play it on the piano. Everyone is in a circle, in wheelchairs, walkers, on crutches, or ambulatory. One person moves around the inside of the circle as all sing:

> As I was walking down the street, down the street, down the street,
> A pretty girl I chanced to meet, heigh-o, heigh-o, heigh-o.

Choose a partner on the last line and both move around the inside of the circle together as all sing chorus:

> Rig-a-jig-jig and away we go, away we go, away we go,
> Rig-a-jig-jig and away we go, heigh-o, heigh-o, heigh-o.

Repeat verse while two people move around the circle single file and choose two new partners. Repeat until everyone has been chosen for partners.

Skip to My Lou: Use a record, or the piano or sing it. Everyone in a single circle, men alternating with ladies. Man has his partner on his right.

> Ladies to the center, skip to my Lou,
> Ladies to the center, skip to my Lou,
> Ladies to the center, skip to my Lou,
> Skip to my Lou, my darling.

On the verse, ladies walk leisurely to the center of the circle, curtsey and walk back to place.

> Gents to the center, skip to my Lou,
> Gents to the center, skip to my Lou,
> Gents to the center, skip to my Lou,
> Skip to my Lou, my darling.

Gents walk into center, bow, and walk back to place.

> Swing your partner, skip to my Lou, etc.

Join both hands with partner and walk around each other.

> Promenade all, skip to my Lou, etc.

Join hands with partner and walk counterclockwise around circle, two by two.

> Lost my partner, what will I do? etc.

Ladies continue walking in direction of promenade while gents turn and walk the opposite way.

> Found another, prettier than you, etc.

Gents find new partner and swing her, then repeat whole dance with the new partner.

Bicycle Built for Two: Sing it, use a piano, or a record if you have one. May be danced with partners anywhere; sitting down, with wheelchairs or walking in a circle with partner.

> Daisy, Daisy, give me your answer true

With right hands joined, walk 8 steps counterclockwise. If seated, hold right hands and bounce up and down 8 times.

I'm half crazy, all for the love of you

Hold left hands, turn and walk clockwise.

It won't be a stylish marriage, I can't afford a carriage

Face partner, shake forefinger and shake head from side to side.

But you'll look sweet upon the seat of a bicycle built for two.

Join both hands and turn partner, if walking. Join both hands and swing them back and forth if sitting.

La Raspa: It is preferable to use a record. This dance can be done with people in bed or wheelchairs as well as ambulatory. For those who are ambulatory, this is a bit strenuous so use discretion.

Stand in a circle, or sit in a circle. Start with the right foot, touching heel on floor forward, then the left heel.

Right, left, right, clap hands twice,
Left, right, left, clap, clap, etc.

On the chorus, hook elbows and skip around each other, changing to left elbows and turning the other way. If seated, hook right elbows and bounce up and down. Repeat with left elbows. Repeat all.

Virgina Reel: Use lively music on record or with a piano. This dance can be done with everyone in wheelchairs, or some in wheelchairs and others walking. It is better to have someone to push the wheelchairs but not necessary if they can propel themselves. Take lots of time for each figure.

Two lines facing about six feet apart. Men are on one side, ladies across. As the lines face the caller the man has his partner on his right.

Bow to partners
Turn partners with right hand around and back to place
Turn partners with left hand and back to place
Turn partners with both hands around and back to place
Do-ci-do partners (back to back, passing right shoulders) and back to place.

Callers may want to skip the "reeling down the center" part if dancers are in wheelchairs and there is a shortage of space.

> All face head of line, and lines separate, ladies to the right, gents to the left, to foot of lines.

First two people make an arch and the others go under with partners and form two lines again. The first couple stays at the foot of the lines.

Square Dancing

Square dancing need not be limited to the traditional four couples in a set or complicated patterns to be fun. Retarded persons can be taught to do simple as well as quite difficult dances if the leader starts with one or two figures and keeps repeating them while adding others. Repetition, economy of words and much demonstration is helpful in teaching the retarded. Persons in wheelchairs can square dance. It is easier if each person in a wheelchair can have someone to push the chair, but some may be able to wheel themselves through the dances. Sitting down square dancing is fun. If possible arrange the dancers in a circle with every other person a man. If there are not enough men (and there never are), pin a crepe paper bow or a ribbon or a hat on the ladies who are being "men." Use lively square dance music and imagination.

The following are suggestions for square dance calls:

All join hands and circle left. (Dancers join hands and lean to the left while bouncing up and down.)

> Circle right.
> Swing partners. (Join both hands and bounce.)
> Swing corners. (Turn to person on the other side and swing.)
> Right hand to partner for an allemande right. (Join right hands and bounce.)
> Left hand to corner for an allemande left.
> Do-ci-do partner. (Touch right shoulders.)
> Do-ci-do corners. (Touch right shoulders with corner.)
> Ladies forward and back. (All ladies lean forward and back.)
> Gents all forward and back. (Men do likewise.)
> Swing corners, swing partners, circle left, circle right, bow to corners, bow to partners, wave to person across the hall, and that's the end of that old call.

Musical Program

A musical program can be very successful. Everyone has an instrument of the "rhythm band." Music should be old time tunes. The director goes to each person not able to get up to "do his thing" and asks him to play his instrument while keeping time to the music. Those able to get up march around the room. The people sitting down do not feel left out when personal attention is given them.

Musical Bingo

Two teams are chosen, with a leader for each team. One team has red cards and the other team has blue cards. A large bingo card is laid on the table or floor. A tune is played on the piano or a record may be used, or the leader may hum the tune. The first team to guess the tune gets to put a card in the space on the big bingo card, where they want it. Continue until one team gets a "bingo." Each person on the team which wins may get a prize.

Chapter 6

FUN WITH NATURE

F UN WITH NATURE is probably the most therapeutic fun of all. The senses of sight, smell, taste, hearing and touch are used in enjoyment of nature but if one or more senses are impaired, the remaining ones can be trained in appreciation of nature.

The bedridden can observe nature through a window or have nature brought to the bedside. Perhaps he can be wheeled on a stretcher to the lawn or porch. Wheelchair patients have unlimited opportunities to enjoy fun with nature. The blind, deaf, paralyzed, paraplegic, nonverbal or other handicapped persons may be recreated through a nature program when all else fails.

A naturalist who visited one mental institution once a month with live animals, birds and nature slides brought about dramatic results. An uncommunicative mentally ill lady laid down on the floor to talk to the baby fox in the cage.

A very elderly bedridden patient, barely alive and unaware of the world around her, lifted her head from the pillow as he showed a raccoon to another patient in the room and said "I never thought that I would live to see a real raccoon."

An adolescent loner became interested in tree identification on nature walks, and now spends many hours walking around the grounds with tree, flower and mushroom books looking for new specimens.

A gallon jar bird feeder still hangs outside the window of an elderly patient in a nursing home and he has become an avid bird watcher.

Patients spent hours watching and talking to the animals and birds which he left at the institution. As he toured the wards showing animals and birds to the patients, this naturalist brought fun with nature to many whose worlds were enclosed within four walls.

There are some ways that everybody can enjoy nature:

1. Keep perfectly still for five minutes and list all of the sounds that you hear.
2. Sit in one spot and make a list of all the trees, birds, flowers and shrubs that you can see and identify.
3. Place a coat hanger upon the ground, sit down beside it and make a list of everything that you find inside it.
4. If ambulatory, throw a stick as far as you can, go to the place where it landed and look for the things that you can identify. The blind can be led to the spot and then identify objects by touch or smell.
5. Have a Sedentary Scavenger Hunt giving each person a list of objects to locate while sitting in one spot. Participants list where the trees, flowers, and other articles are. For example, gray squirrel's nest; in maple tree near the fountain. The first person to complete the list wins a wheelchair ride to the Canteen for an ice cream cone.
6. Have a Feel-a-vision Contest. With eyes closed, how many trees can you identify by feeling the bark, leaves or needles. Or have a Smell-a-vision Contest to determine who can identify the most flowers, trees or plants by smelling blossoms, crushed leaves or needles.
7. Have the patients plant a garden. Individual flower gardens can be staked off on a larger plot of ground. Let each choose a packet of seeds to plant. The patients can be taken from time to time to water and weed the gardens, and later to harvest the vegetables or pick the flowers.

   If patients cannot go outdoors, they can have individual window boxes, or a potted plant beside their beds. (Check agency rules about this!)
8. Take nature walks or hikes and look for flowers, trees, plants and birds that the group cannot identify. Look them up in guide books.

9. Lay out a nature trail around the grounds with identification tags on trees, shrubs and plants. Make a smooth path so that wheelchairs can be pushed along it and folks with canes or walkers can take short walks. Use the existing sidewalks, driveways and other paths and identify the trees and flowers along the way.

10. Make terrariums and aquariums for day rooms in the institution.

11. Have a Nature Bulletin Board in the recreation room or dayrooms. Put different leaves, barks, wood or other objects on it each day and have a contest to see how many people can identify them. Have a "mystery corner" on the bulletin board and put a real difficult nature specimen there to identify.

12. Have nature quizzes. Divide the group into teams as they are sitting on a porch, lawn, around a campfire or even in the dayroom of the institution. The leader may ask questions like "Where do woodpeckers build their nests?" or "Are termites insects?" or "How can you tell a red pine from a white pine?" The person giving the correct answer first gets a point for his team. The leader had better know the answers before he asks the questions.

13. Take a short nature walk, even a wheelchair nature walk, telling everyone to watch along the way for something of special interest. After the group has returned to the starting point, have a discussion about what was seen or heard.

Some nature games to play are as follows:

Prove It

The players sit in a circle. The one starting the game says "From where I sit I can see a gray birch." The next person says "From where I sit I can see a gray birch and a white maple." The next person repeats all that the previous persons have said and adds another tree or flower or bird. If anyone doubts that the person can see what he says he can, he may challenge the person to point it out. Anyone caught who is unable to prove that he can see what he says he can see is disqualified from the game.

Fetch It

The players are divided into two teams, lined up in relay fashion, one behind another. The leader asks the first person on each team to "fetch" one cluster of needles from a red pine, or some other object. The first person to get back with it gets one point for his team. Both players go to the end of the line. The leader then asks the next two to fetch something else, like a maple leaf.

The leader may assign an article to each person on the team before the game starts, then as soon as the first person returns with his object, the next person in line runs to fetch his. The line getting all players back first, wins.

I Spy

The players may be sitting on the lawn or resting on a hike. The leader may say "I spy a robin's nest." As each person spies the nest, he holds up his hand. All those who spy the nest in a given time, like two minutes, get a point. Then choose another leader, who may say "'I spy a gray squirrel."

Take trips to museums which are available in many communities; a fish hatchery; local, state and national forests and parks; farms, because many city people have never seen one; a wildlife area such as a swamp, pond, field, forest or game preserve; local fish and game club areas; zoos and animal farms.

Resource people who can help you are game wardens, county foresters and extension agents, naturalists, nature photographers, zoo keepers, Fish and Game departments, local science teachers, state and national recreation agencies, National Wildlife Society, Audubon societies, libraries and other agencies.

Some nature projects that you might do are as follows:

1. Study aphids, ants and other insects. Small colonies can be set up in gallon glass jars to be watched.
2. Hollow out a carrot and hang it up by its tail in a window. Fill it with water and watch it grow. Do the same with a sweet potato.

3. Make maps of a nature area which is nearby, or of the institution grounds, marking where the most interesting trees, wild flowers, bird nests and other things are located.

4. Have a pet show or a turtle race, frog race or snail race. Get out publicity and talk it up. Have each person catch his own "racer" and hold trial runs. Set up some rules to protect the pets.

5. Make collections of leaves, wood samples, insects, rocks, dried wild flowers, or other nature objects.

6. Plant flowers in an area that needs beautifying. Bring in wild flowers and make a garden. Check carefully to determine what flowers can be transplanted easily and which are protected by law against picking.

7. Make posters to promote fire prevention, conservation, prevention of cruelty to animals, preservation of vanishing wildlife or antipollution.

8. Make a scrapbook of flower, animal, bird or tree pictures with identification.

9. Write and produce a short play about nature.

10. Have an essay contest on a nature subject, like conservation.

11. Invite a nature photographer to give an illustrated lecture.

12. Build and put up bird houses. Plant shrubs for food and cover for the birds.

13. Learn to identify edible plants and how to prepare them to eat.

14. Make aquariums and terrariums.

15. Make plaster casts of animal tracks.

16. Make drawings or sketches or paintings of plants, animals or landscapes.

17. Do some nature crafts.

18. Play a game, sing a song, have fun with nature.

Nature Prints

Place ferns, leaves, sprigs of fir, grasses or other objects on a sheet of construction paper. Arrange them in any design which you like. Pin them with straight pins so that they will not become disarranged when sprayed. If you place the construction paper over several layers of newspapers, it is easier to stick in the pins.

Holding a can of spray paint (gold, silver, bronze or whatever color you want) about eighteen inches away from the picture, spray paint over the arrangement. After the paint has dried, remove the pins and the other objects from the paper. The leaves, ferns or whatever you used will be covered with paint and after drying may be mounted on a sheet of paper, piece of burlap, or black velvet and framed to make a lovely picture.

Frames around the nature prints may be done easily by tacking a strip of paper around the edge of the print before it is sprayed.

Seed Mosaics

Mosaics can be made from seeds, bits of cones, dried peas, beans and corn, pebbles, broken glass, bits of ceramic tile or just about anything that can be glued to another surface. Mosaics made from natural materials are attractive and inexpensive. Seeds, seed pods and pebbles can be found anywhere.

Outline the design on a piece of stiff cardboard or poster board or a piece of weathered board with a pencil. Apply a quick-drying glue where you want the seeds to be. Then sprinkle on the seeds and allow the glue to dry. Shake off the excess materials. Use different seeds or cones to achieve a variety of design. Cover with two thin coats of clear shellac or other transparent finish when completed.

Owl Portraits

Draw the outline of an owl on a sheet of heavy cardboard or other heavy material. Break pine or spruce cones into individual bits which look like feathers. Coat the areas to be feathered with glue, then with tweezers or small pliers, or fingers if manually dexterous, place the cone petals on these areas. Start at the bottom and work up so that the feathers overlap. Use felt for eyes, beak and feet, or you can use dried corn, peas and beans. Frame the completed picture and hang it on the wall.

Pebble Zoo

Take some nature walks along an area where there is a supply of pebbles and small stones. A riverbed or gravel pit are likely spots. Pick up pebbles that have interesting shapes which might be used for bodies or heads of birds and animals. Take them back to the craft room, and with epoxy glue, assemble the stones to look like animals or birds. A little paint, bits of felt, leather or other materials may be added for features. Put them in little cages and have a zoo.

Woodland Terrariums

Find a glass container with a cover. A fish tank or a gallon jar may be used. Clean it and place clean gravel on the bottom to the depth of an inch or two for drainage. Press small pieces of charcoal into the gravel then cover with one or two inches of slightly sandy humus that has been dampened. Spread leaf mold over the humus. Do not make the surface level but leave some little hills and valleys. Find small ferns, mosses, tiny tree seedlings, wintergreen or partridge berries, ground pine and other plants found in woodland areas. Add a small rock or two with lichen growing on it.

Cover the terrarium and keep in a cool spot with good light but not bright sunlight. If moisture gathers on the inside of the terrarium, take off the cover until it evaporates. It should not need watering more than once a month.

Cages for Small Live Things

Almost anything which can be kept dry and which is transparent can be used. Large mouth gallon jars are always available from the kitchen. Cover the top with a piece of cloth held with a rubber band and you have a cage.

Cocoons and chrysalises may be collected to watch while they are pupating. Take eight or ten inches of the branch upon which the cocoon is attached. Place the branch in a gallon jug with cloth over the top so that the cocoon is in about the same position as you found it. It should not be resting against anything. The cocoon or chrysalis should be sprinkled lightly three or four times a week, but do not soak. Watch them hatch into lovely butterflies, or maybe just lots of flies.

Crickets and grasshoppers can be kept in an aquarium, terrarium or wide mouth jar. Cover the top with cloth. At least two inches of damp soil with flat stone and a few twigs should be placed in the container. Keep a piece of moistened cotton in the cage at all times, but the soil should never be very wet. Put a bottle cap filled with water in the cage for drinking. Grasshoppers need fresh green grass daily. Crickets will eat bits of fruit and vegetables. Small pieces of apple will supply them with food. Try different foods to see what they like.

If a female cricket should be observed laying eggs into the soil, turn her loose, sprinkle grass seed on the bottom of the cage, water it occasionally and when the baby crickets hatch, green grass will be growing for them to eat.

Bird Feeders to Make

Donut Ring: The materials needed are a zinc coat hanger and stale doughnuts. Form the hanger into a circle. Cut one side of the wire where it joins the hook. Bend about one-half inch of this free end in a "U" so that it can be hooked to the other side. Thread stale doughnuts onto the circle and hang it on a tree limb.

Pie Tin Feeder: A small aluminum pie plate and a short dowel are the materials needed to form this feeder. Melt suet in a double boiler. Fill the pie plate half full of mixed bird seed. Pour melted suet over this until the pie plate is filled. Before the mixture hardens, thrust the dowel into the bottom to serve as a perch for the birds. When hard, hang with a length of wire.

Suet Stick: Needed is a small log, three to four inches in diameter and twelve to fifteen inches long. Drill one and a half inch holes one inch deep into the log in about a dozen places. Fill the holes with suet or peanut butter and hang it on a tree limb where it can be found by woodpeckers, nuthatches and chickadees. (When feeding homogenized peanut butter, mix in dry bread crumbs or corn meal until mixture is crumbly. Birds will choke to death on plain homogenized peanut butter.)

Pine Cone Feeder: The materials needed are a pine cone (pitch pine preferably), and a piece of fine wire. Wrap the wire around the tip of the pine cone so that it can be hung upside down. Fill the spaces between the scales with peanut butter and hang it on a tree limb.

Flower Pot Feeder: The materials needed for this project are a small flower pot, length of dowel and a clip-type clothes pin. Push the dowel through the hole in the bottom of the flower pot and hold it in place with a cotter pin or bent nail. Screw or wire the clip-type clothes pin to upper end of the dowel. Fill the flower pot with mixed seed or sunflower seed and clip to a tree branch.

Milk Carton Feeder: The only item needed for this feeder is an empty milk carton. Starting about one and a half inches from the bottom of the carton cut out the opposite sides. Fill the bottom with mixed seed or sunflower seed and hang with a length of wire.

Chapter 7

FUN WITH CRAFTS

C RAFTS FOR FUN can be anything from hand-tooled leather to egg shell mosaics, intricate wood carving to string weaving, pottery turned on a potter's wheel to papier-mâché modeling. The important thing is that the finished product be something that a person has created with his own hands. To others it may be not quite perfect but to the creator it is "his thing" even though badly painted, crooked, cracked or warped. Every person who wishes should be given the opportunity to create, whether that person be blind, deaf, handicapped or healthy.

The good leader provides the materials and encouragement and the opportunity to create. The crafts program can be conducted anywhere, on a bedside table, in the dining room around tables, in a wheelchair with a lap board, or a well-equipped craft room. The imaginative leader will find ways to help the more severely handicapped to create. The finished product may be sold, given as a gift or displayed on the creator's dresser.

Things to Collect and Save

Aluminum foil	Milk cartons
Bottles	Lace
Buttons	Plastic bottles
Cardboard	Paper bags
Construction paper	Ribbon
Greeting cards	Shoe boxes
Jewelry	Yarn
Felt and cloth scrap	Pencils
Glue	String
Paint	Spools
Styrofoam balls	Pipe cleaners
Flash cubes	Magazines
Coat hangers	Popsickle sticks
Crayons	Toothbrushes

SOME "CRAFTY" IDEAS

Decorated Cans

Empty play dough cans can be covered easily using colored medium Bond paper and Elmer's glue. Cans can then be decorated and used for pencils, paint brushes, or other odds and ends. Take a sheet of paper, fold in half lengthwise, place around the can with the folded edge meeting the rim on the bottom of the can. The top edge is folded in. Possibilities for decorating cans are unlimited.

Greeting Cards

Children in our pediatric section bring cheer to all departments at holiday time. All persons who send gifts to the wards receive a special thank you card. All cards are made by the children with the help of the teacher. Since every card is a pediatric "original" the name "Pedioriginal" appears on the back of each card.

White preglued paper is used. The edges are pinked.

Party Favors

Materials: Cardboard tubes 4½ inches long; lightweight paper, any color; plastic Baggies, sandwich size; elastic band; animal pattern or cutout or picture; paste, scissors, ruler; crayons.

Directions: Insert Baggie into tube. Fold over one inch of the Baggie to the outside of the tube, and secure with the rubber band. Cover the tube with paper. Various cutouts of animals can be used for decorating the outside. The favor will stand as an attractive place marker.

Butterfly

Materials: One piece of 8½ x 11 lightweight paper in a light shade or white, crayons, yarn, one 12 inch pipe cleaner, preferably colored.

Directions: Have children color both sides of paper with circles and lines. The three-year-old child can do this well. The leader can help younger children with folding the paper, which is done with an accordian pleat. When completed, the butterfly has a width of about one inch. Find the middle of the pleated paper. Fold the pipe cleaner around once and then twist until secure. Separate the folds so the colors show. Tie a string around the pipe cleaner loop. Twirl the completed butterfly overhead and watch it fly.

Ceramic tile work (trivets, flower pots, table tops), liquid embroidery, pillows and small animal stuffing and library service can be done by the senile, aging and physically handicapped.

Creative Wall Plaques

This is a very easy project where everyone can be successful. Even though it is a very simple project, those with imagination and talent can produce very intricate and creative plaques.

Materials: Pieces of pine or other soft wood 6 inches x 4 inches x 1 inch, chisel, plaster and a plastic or rubber bowl, brushes and poster paint, varnish, wood stain, nails, sandpaper, wall hanging hook.

Directions: Chisel out from the center of the pine block a hole about 4 inches x 3 inches x ½ inch. The block then needs to be sanded and the corners rounded. After sanding, the plaster is prepared in a flexible bowl. Fill the bowl about two inches with water. Sift in the plaster through your fingers slowly until a mound is formed in the middle of the water and about half an inch above the water level. Mix the plaster and water. Fill the hole in the pine block with the plaster. Smooth the plaster and wipe away the excess. Let the plaster begin to harden ten or fifteen minutes or until it does not look watery. Then draw a picture using the nail in the plaster. This picture can be as simple as a piece of fruit or as complex as a mosaic design. Let the plaster dry overnight. The next day, sand off the rough plaster. Paint the picture and stain the wood. Let it dry. Finally, varnish the plaster and wood and attach the hanging hook.

A Party Tablecloth

This project is essentially good for a new group that needs to work together. It not only encourages them to work together but also gives them a chance to compare their skills and to feel satisfaction by contributing to a larger project. It is also fun.

There is a variety of ways to make the tablecloth. This is an easy method. Let your imagination go and adapt it to your group.

Materials: A large piece of burlap, felt in a large variety of colors, coloring books for patterns, scissors, glue, wool fringe long enough to edge the burlap.

Directions: Roll the burlap or felt on to a large table and sit your group around it. First, discuss what the people want on the tablecloth. Do they want just Christmas decorations, fruit, flowers or a variety of patterns which would make the table-cloth suitable for every holiday and party. The group can find the patterns in the coloring books and cut the felt into these patterns. Every person is to decorate at least the portion of the cloth in front of him by gluing his felt patterns to the burlap. When all the patterns are securely on the cloth and the decorators are happy with the design, the fringe can be sewed to the edges of the cloth. The project is complete and the participants have had fun as well as creating a pretty and useful object.

Luigi

Materials: Old bottle, styrofoam ball for head, masking tape, felt for clothes and features, acrylic paint (make your own with Elmer's glue and poster paint), 20 gauge wire, yarn, papier mâché (commercial or make your own), and spray lacquer for sealing.

Directions: Wash and clean the bottle. Glue the cap to the styrofoam ball and let it dry. Cover the bottle with masking tape. With the wire, attach pieces for arms and bend the ends for hands. Cover the bottle with papier mâché, including arms and hands. Cover the styrofoam head with it, forming the nose and rest of features. Let it dry thoroughly. Cut the felt and glue it on for clothes. Cut the yarn the desired length for hair.

Magazine Christmas Wreath

Use a *Look* or *Life* magazine. Fold one page in half length-wise. Cut the folded page in one inch cuts. Turn outside in, fold in three and staple. Cut a piece of cardboard into a circle ten inches or so in diameter. Place the paper pom-pom on the outer edge of the circle and staple. Complete all around edge. Overlap half of the next row about three rows. Work towards the inner edge. Spray paint the wreath any color and sprinkle with glitter. Add a ribbon bow if you wish.

Rice or Eggshell Mosaics

Materials: Rice or eggshells, Elmer's glue, construction paper, cardboard or an article to be covered.

Directions: Use Easter egg dye or crepe paper. Hot water from the tap can be used with the crepe paper. Use a gallon can, drop the crepe paper into the hot water, add the egg shells and leave until dark enough or the water is cold, then spread out on newspaper to dry. When crisp, roll with anything convenient and store in bottles or tin cans. They can be dried more quickly in an oven.

Use the egg shells to make simple silhouettes on cardboard, outlines, simple pictures from coloring books, or abstract design on plates, bottles, boxes or other articles.

Dyed Macaroni

Add pure food coloring to nontoxic rubbing alcohol to obtain the desired pastel or deep shade of color. Pour into the alcohol a quantity of alphabet macaroni and various sizes and shapes of macaroni. Allow to set for thirty seconds, then pour off the alcohol. Spread the macaroni out to dry. It may be used for stringing beads, making name labels, or decorating boxes, bottles and other articles.

Coat Hanger Crafts

Wire coat hangers can be shaped to make many things like broomholders, toasting forks for hotdogs, flower pot wall holders, newspaper racks, or just art forms to be mounted on a block of wood.

Paper Bag Masks

Put paper bag over the head and mark where the eyes are.

With a crayon, draw in the features of a face. Paste on nose, ears, eyelashes, hair made of yarn or paper, and cut the eye holes part way out. Lift them up to see. Use imagination!

Toys from Boxes

Cars, trucks and trains can be made from match boxes, cigar boxes, cheese or milk cartons, bottle tops, oatmeal boxes, match sticks and paint. Use different size boxes for the cab and trailer of the trucks, bottle caps for wheels, match sticks for steering rod and a small bottle cap for the steering wheel. A good activity for children of all ages.

Peep Shows

Materials: A shoe box, cigar box or any durable box which may be used to hold the Peep Show. The scene inside may be cut from magazines, comic books, drawn with crayons, or objects may be used to give a 3-D effect. Some paste, scissors and colored paper is all that is required.

Directions: The side walls of the box may be decorated to provide a setting. Place the objects to make the scene on the bottom of the box. Cut holes in the cover of the box with colored paper pasted over them. Be sure that the right colored light shines on the objects made. Cut peepholes in the sides or the ends of the box.

Decorated Notepaper

Use plain notepaper which comes with envelopes to fit. Arrange ferns, dried flowers, grasses, leaves or pictures cut from magazines on the front of the notepaper. Cut a piece of transparent contact paper the same size as the notepaper and place very gently over the design. Press down until it adheres to the paper.

String Cages

Prepare a mixture of half wallpaper paste and half laundry starch. Tie blown up balloons to a rack so that they hang freely. Oil them with salad oil. Draw string or yarn through the paste mixture until it is thoroughly dampened. Wind it around the balloon, crisscrossing in every direction, leaving a window at the top of the balloon. When the yarn has dried thoroughly, burst the balloon and take out the pieces. Spray the cages with paint, and glitter over dabs of Elmer's glue. Suspend small birds, sprigs of green, ornaments or other objects inside.

Pomanders

Materials: One 2 inch styrofoam ball; a package of 1½ inch hairpins, silver or light colored; one quarter of a yard of nylon net of one color and another quarter of a yard of another color; six small flowers; whole cloves; 12 inches of one-half inch ribbon to match the net.

Directions: Using the length of nylon as it comes from the bolt, fold twice lengthwise dividing folded net into thirds. Make cross cuts 4 inches apart. Cut all folds, leaving rectangles of 4 inches x 5 inches. Fold one rectangle lengthwise and gather on one prong of the hairpin. Pull gathered net to the curve of the hairpin. Push hairpin into styrofoam ball. Continue this process using alternate colors until ball is covered. Add one flower to the center of six tufts, add ten or twelve cloves and some of the green leaves cut from the flowers, insert at random. Tie ends of 12 inches of ribbon together, insert prong of hairpin in knot and then insert into styrofoam ball for a hanger.

Christmas Quickies

Cut out single sections of egg cartons, spray with gold paint, add glitter, beads or other decorations and hang on the Christmas tree.

Paper Doily Snowflakes: Staple eight paper doilies together across the center. Hang by a ribbon.

Bouncing Snowballs: Put the following in an attractive jar or bowl:

> 1 cup water
> ⅓ cup vinegar
> 1 teaspoon baking powder
> 5 moth balls

The moth balls bounce up and down in the solution for five or six hours.

Paper Bag Reindeer: Cut the head of the reindeer out of one paper bag. Color and glue on the front of another paper bag. The reindeer can be placed over bottles, cans or boxes for a Christmas wrapping decoration.

Flash Bulb Ornaments: Decorate flash bulb cubes with spray paint, glitter, beads or other decorations. Hang them on the Christmas tree.

Santa Jars: Use Laredo cigarette and tobacco cans. Cover with red paper, contact paper, red felt or paint. Decorate to look like Santa with top half serving as top of Santa's face. Fill the can with cookies or candy.

Felt Heads: Cut out round pieces of felt for heads. Make a face on one with small bits of felt, beads, buttons or sequins. Glue two together over the eraser end of a pencil to make a head.

Rolled Magazine Pages

Basic materials: dowels, several sizes, each about a foot long; old magazines or catalogs; Scotch tape, Elmer's glue; scissors; ice cream cartons; poster board; and shirt cardboards.

Rolling Method: Roll diagonally around a dowel, or a pencil may be used, and secure with Scotch tape. If a magazine, the pages are torn out and the edges usually need to be trimmed before rolling.

To make a waste basket use a three gallon ice cream carton. Wash it out and dry it, put a small bead of glue the full length of the rolled page and stick on to the carton vertically. Continue around the carton until it is completely covered. The carton may be finished off with varnish or shellac both inside and out. Also, cartons covered with wallpaper samples make attractive waste baskets.

Additional Ideas

Pictures from magazine or calendars may be mounted on heavy cardboard then cut into puzzles.

Greetings cards (used) may be made into place cards or other greeting cards.

Papier mâché is easily made by tearing newspaper into tiny bits and soaking the paper before adding glue or homemade paste. This type of pulp is used for modeling.

Bowls and trays may be made by using strips of paper and a bowl or tray used as a mold. The pieces are soaked, then dipped into paste or glue and applied, one at a time. As soon as the article is dried, it may be sanded before paint is applied.

Wallpaper sample books (with large pieces) may be used to cover waste basket and boxes for gift wrapping or for greeting cards.

Small flat wooden boxes of varying depths and lengths may be nailed together and stained or painted to serve as shelves for miniatures.

Broom and mop handles make footstools and table legs.

A practical garden refreshment stand requires one broom handle, pointed on the end. The top is made into an oval or round shape from an orange crate or other wooden box.

Berry boxes may be painted and used as gift containers for candy, cookies or other things. These may be lined and used as knitting bags.

Blanket strips may be used for hooked, braided or crocheted rugs.

Coarse net samples may be decorated with darned designs for mats and scarves.

Large sweaters may be ravelled, then the yarn damp rewound and used again.

Knit work socks can be used after the feet are worn out. Cut the top into strips about an inch wide and use the loops for weaving potholders.

Modeling Materials

Modeling Dough: Mix one cup of salt, one half cup of cornstarch, and two thirds of a cup of water. Cook over low heat, stirring constantly until it is a thick, doughy mass. Remove from stove and cool. If colors are desirable, separate and knead in various vegetable colors. Roll into a ball for storing, wrap in waxed paper or a plastic bag and keep cool, preferably in the refrigerator. The dough can be rolled into small balls and a hole made through them with a toothpick. When dry they can be strung for beads. The dough can also be made into dishes and many other articles.

Play Dough: Mix one cup of salt, one cup of flour and slowly add one cup of water. If stored in a tightly closed container, it can be used over and over again.

Additional recipes:

1 pint of sawdust
1 pint   plaster of Paris
¼ pint library paste

Add enough water to paste to make it thin and runny. Stir in plaster, then sawdust, and knead to a doughy consistency. It hardens in fifteen or twenty minutes.

2 pints wet newspaper pulp
1 pint plaster of Paris
¼ teaspoon LePage's glue
½ pint water

Make pulp by soaking newspaper for several hours then rub between hands. Add the glue to the water. Stir in plaster and then paper pulp. Knead to a doughy consistency. This formula takes about three hours to harden.

½ pint wet newspaper pulp
½ pint sifted, powdered dry clay
1 teaspoon LePage's glue
1 cup of water

Dissolve glue in water and add dry clay. Stir well and add wet paper pulp. Knead to a heavy doughy consistency. Allow about twelve hours to dry.

1 pint sawdust
¾ pint plaster of Paris
½ pint library paste
3 drops LePage's glue

Dissolve paste in water to thin. Add glue. Stir in plaster then sawdust. Knead to a heavy consistency. Allow about eight hours to harden.

2 pints wet newspaper pulp
2 pints plaster of Paris
¼ teaspoon LePage's glue
½ pint water

Add glue to water. Stir in plaster then add paper pulp. Stir in plaster then add paper pulp. Knead to a doughy consistency. Allow about 30 minutes to harden.

Patchwork Painting

A Patchwork Painting is an artist's canvas stretched over a frame with squares marked off in which artists, amateurs, professionals and children fill in a square of their own choosing with whatever subject they wish.

This was done in the 1961 Sidewalk Art Show in Concord, New Hampshire. Ninety 5 inch x 7 inch squares were to be filled. Viewers of the exhibit, whether residents or just passing through, were invited to perform their artistic abilities on the canvas. Most artists chose to fill only one square, where another artist used up to five squares for a portrait. All ages and all talents worked to complete the canvas. A portrait beside an abstract, a snow scene next to a colorful field of wheat, the face of a child lovingly painted above a still life of fruit. Brushes, pallet knives and even fingers were used in the creation.

On the playground, a contest is held in which each park makes their Patchwork Painting with tempera paints on poster board and displays them at the Sidewalk exhibit. The children are careful of subject and continuity, for judges are appointed to choose the best to be exhibited in the Community Center for the coming year.

Have an Art Show

Prepare "genius kits" consisting of canvas (any textured fabric stapled on to a heavy cardboard), a cigar or candy box containing a variety of precut felt and lengths of varicolored wools and any other scrap items like stones, buttons, beads, and a tube of art glue that can be used with one hand and dries clear.

Gather the artists and explain the project with the aid of several demonstration masterpieces. Give out the genius kits. Provide an approximate time limit of 30 minutes for each to complete his canvas.

Stand the works of art in a row where all can see them and have a judging with ribbons for the winners. It is fun to have coffee or punch to serve as contestants finish so your art show ends as a social experience and everyone is a winner. Hang the art works in the dining room or lounge.

Chapter 8

FUN WITH GAMES

THE GAMES PEOPLE PLAY are many and varied, quiet or active, highly organized or low organized or hardly organized at all. They can be equipment games, mental games, musical games, team games, table games, indoor games or outdoor games. Games can be played with many people or just one or two. Games can be played by anybody, anywhere at any time.

Many leaders in recreation programs for the ill, handicapped or aging do not feel comfortable about leading games. They have many excuses, such as "the patients are too sick, or too old, or too young, or too regressed, retarded or handicapped, too this or too that." The real reason may be that the leader has never led a game or perhaps never played a game, and is afraid to move out of more familiar areas like crafts.

Everybody can lead a game and get the participants to enjoy playing it. A positive attitude toward games is the first prerequisite. Never ask "Do you want to play a game?" because probably at least half of the group will reply "No." Just give the rules as quickly and clearly as possible with the assumption that everyone is going to play, and start playing the game. Be prepared to accept some nonparticipation without getting discouraged. How many leaders are the first on their feet when a game is introduced at a party which they may be fortunate enough to attend when someone else is the leader?

If people are in a room where games are being played, they are participating even though they are just sitting and watching.

Know the game well before you try to lead it. Nothing is more disastrous than to have the leader forget the rules when everyone is poised to play.

Devise adaptations to games so that *all* can play. This comes from experience. Help the poorly coordinated throw a beanbag by holding his or her hand in yours and giving a little push.

Know when to encourage the participants to play a game and when to let them watch. If a person strikes the leader after too much encouragement, he may assume that he has pushed too far!

Use common sense about the games you choose for people to play. Obviously, the leader will not plan an hour of active games for a group of cardiac patients. Neither is the perceptive leader going to plan several running relays for the players who are in wheelchairs or walkers. But one or two such games can be played by slowing them down to their players' speed.

Games requiring sight would not be planned for a party for the blind, and games requiring the ability to hear would not be played with the deaf. On the other hand, the leader should not eliminate all opportunities for the handicapped to use the abilities which they still possess. The partially paralyzed can figure out how to throw or catch a beanbag or ball if given a chance. The blind can play the same games as the sighted if you explain what the game is and stand in front of the target, bowling pins, or other scoring area and talk.

People who are sick or paralyzed or blind or deaf or old or mentally retarded or mentally ill or otherwise incapacitated have not lost the ability to have fun playing games. With more time on their hands, they can enjoy playing games more than when they were "well."

The experienced leader who conducts games in a therapeutic setting devises many little gimmicks to help people enjoy more the game that they play. Some of these leaders have shared their successes with other leaders who are toiling in the vineyard. This chapter includes a few of them. Try them. They may work for you, too!

Huckle, Buckle Beanstock

Any number of people can play. A small object is used that can be hidden. Everyone must be shown what it is before the game starts. One player is "It." Others go out of the room or cover their eyes. "It" hides the object in the room in sight but not too obvious to those entering the room. "It" calls "OK" to other players who enter in search of the object. They are told they are "hot" (near the object) or "cold" (far from the object). As soon as a player sees the hidden object, he says "Huckle, Buckle Beanstock" and sits down. He must not touch the object. Other players continue to hunt for the object until they all have located it. The first player who found the object is the next to hide it.

Loop the Legs

Get a pair of plastic women's legs (the kind that can be inflated) from a joke shop. Blow them up and stick them in a cardboard carton, feet up. Put a pair of nurse's shoes on the feet. The patients throw embroidery hoops at the feet and try to loop them over. Players get five points for each hoop that loops a foot.

Narts

Draw the face of a nurse with cap on a large piece of cardboard. Give the players darts to throw at the face. Scoring is five points for an eye, ten points for a nose, and fifteen points for the mouth. A prize is given to the high scorer.

Rock the Nurse Party

A face is painted on a styrofoam head form and a wig added with a nurse's cap on the head. The patients throw beanbags at the head and those knocking the head over get a prize. The patients enjoy "rocking the nurse" and almost everyone, even the weakest, can win prizes.

Live Tic-Tac Toe

Two teams are used and may be men against the women, a circle of people divided, or half of the group wearing crepe paper bows. One team is the "X's'" and the other team the "O's." This can be indicated by crossing the arms to make an X or making a circle with arms for the O. Arrange nine chairs in rows of three like a tic-tac-toe game on paper. A leader for each team gives the directions and the game is played like it is on paper with three in a row alike winning.

The leader tells the "X" where to sit, then the other leader tells an "O" where to sit and so on until the nine chairs are filled. If there are not three of a kind in a row, the "cat" gets the game. Choose another captain for each team and play again. This game can be played with people in wheelchairs by making the squares on the floor with chalk and wheeling the chairs into the squares.

Hot Potato

Seat the players in a circle. The leader puts a lively record on the record player or someone plays the piano. Use any object for passing. A large plastic ball or a beanbag is best for people who have difficulty holding articles. While the music is playing, the article is passed from person to person to the right. When it stops, the person holding it has a point against him or pays a forfeit or has a small clothespin clipped on to his collar to show that he has been caught. Start the music and continue passing the object. This game can be adapted to holidays by making the object a "heart" or a "skull" or a "shamrock" or a "reindeer." This game always works with any age group.

Table Top Quoits

Get some rubber jar rings to use for quoits, and pound a nail into a piece of board for a peg. Stand one at either end of a table or place one on the floor in front of players or put it on a bed. Players score five points for each ringer that they make by throwing the jar rings over the pegs.

Snowball Fight

Each person is given a full sheet of newspaper. At a signal each uses just one hand and tries to crumple the paper into the smallest possible wad. These paper balls become snowballs and at a signal, both teams start throwing the snowballs at each other. When the signal is given to stop, each side counts the snowballs on its side. The side with the fewest snowballs wins.

Balloon Swat

Each player is given a rolled newspaper for a swatter. A

balloon with a piece of string is tied to the player's waist in back or to the arm of a wheelchair. Players all are arranged in a circle to start. At the signal, everyone moves around and starts swatting other balloons to break them while guarding his own at the same time. As soon as a player's ballon is broken, he is out of the game. The player who stays in the game the longest gets to keep his balloon for a prize.

Discus Throw

Contestants write their names on paper plates and all stand behind the starting line and try to sail the plates through the air to an opposite line. The plate going the greatest distance wins.

Balloon Bat

Contestants line up behind designated starting lines, in two teams. A chair or other goal post is set up at the opposite side of the room or playing area. At the starting signal, first players on each team start batting the balloons with open hands to the goal, around it, and back to the starting line. As soon as the first player returns the balloon, he goes to the end of the line and the next person starts batting the balloon around the goal. The first team to get all players back first wins the game. Players in wheelchairs can play this game, as well as those on crutches. But have all players in wheelchairs or of equal mobility.

Badminton Birdie Throw

Players stand or sit behind a line and throw a badminton "birdie" as far as they can throw it. Give a small prize to the one who throws it the farthest. Or give each player in turn a badminton racket, and the leader tosses the birdie to the player who has three chances to hit it. This is fun and good exercise for arms.

Playing Card Toss

The player holding a number of playing cards, sits on a chair. A few feet in front of him is a wastebasket, or other receptacle, into which he tries to toss the cards one at a time.

The whole deck of cards may be used, but there should be at least twenty. They should be thrown rapidly. The player who gets the most cards in the receptacle wins. This could also be a game of solitaire for one player.

Deuce to Ace Race

The contestants sit at a table or may use any other play area. Each player has a complete deck of cards, well shuffled. At a signal, each player starts to arrange his cards by suit and rank. The cards are to be made into single piles running from the deuce up to the ace in each suit. The first to arrange his cards in four piles in proper order wins the game.

Tearable Occupations

Give each player a piece of paper and ask him to tear out some symbol of his occupation or hobby. These are pinned on the front of each person and others try to guess what the occupation is.

Count Up

Two players play the game. The object of the game is to be the one to say "twenty." They take turns saying numbers and may say one but not more than two at a time. For example, the first player may say "one"; the second player "two, three," and so on. After the players have been through the numbers a few times they will figure out which numbers they want to say in order to be the one to get "twenty."

Musical Balloon Bounce

Players are seated around tables. Each table has a large inflated balloon. While music is playing, players hit the balloon back and forth, keeping it in the air. When the music stops, the balloon must be caught immediately and placed on the table. The last table to catch the balloon has one point scored against it. If the group breaks the balloon, that table is out of the game.

Secret Objects

Players may be seated around tables. Each player is asked

to select something small that he is wearing or has in his pocket
and to hold it in his hand. At a given signal, everyone places
his object on the table in front of him. A scorekeeper at each
table scores the objects as follows:

10 points for every different item

10 points for every pair of similar things

10 points for anything red

25 points for a Good Luck piece

10 points for every watch with a second hand

25 points for sets of triplets

Lay all items together end to end in the longest line possible and measure length of each line. The total number of inches
is the score.

10 points for edible items

10 points for items with precious stones

10 points for handmade items

Pile up the articles and give ten points for the smallest pile.
At a signal, all grab articles back and stand up. 10 points
for the table whose players stand first.

100 or 1

Two to six or more people can play this game. One player
begins by throwing a die as many times as he wants, building
up his score by adding the numbers thrown. His aim is to go as
high as he can without throwing the number 1. If he throws
this, he scores zero for this turn (not his accumulated score)
and gives the die to the next person on his left. Each player
who reaches a score of 100 is a winner.

Passball

Players are in a circle and pass a ball at random about
the circle. The leader, with his back to the circle, blows a
whistle from time to time. Whoever is holding the ball is elimi-
nated from that game, or may have one point scored against
him. If eliminating the players, play until only one person is
left in the game. More than one ball may be used.

What is it?

Collect several interesting, unusual items and put them into a "mystery box." The leader looks into the box and chooses one article without removing it. The players ask questions about the object until one guesses what it is. Also, tape unusual articles like an old shoe button hook, on to separate pieces of cardboard and pass them around for people to identify. Articles may also be tacked to pieces of heavy cloth with stout thread. This game generates much conversation, especially amongst older people, if articles which they used in the "old days" are passed around.

Famous Folks Faces

Cut from magazines or newspapers the faces of people that everyone is likely to know. Paste them to separate sheets of paper. To make the game more difficult, cut out one feature, like the nose. Pass them around for players to identify, or tack them up on the bulletin board and let the residents have a guessing game for several days. Slips of paper might be provided for their answers to be written on and placed in a box. Or put a numbered sheet under each picture and let the players sign their names and the name of the person whom they think it is. Advertisements, comic strip characters and other pictures may also be used.

Deer and Rabbit

Players work with partners for this stunt. A penny is fastened to a 12 inch length of string with a piece of tape or some glue. The coin should be taped to hang vertically, and a knot or two may be tied in the other end of the string. One player holds the string so that the penny hangs an inch or two over the outstretched palm of the other player. Both think "deer" and how it usually moves in a straight line when running. The coin will soon begin to swing forward and back. Then think "rabbit" and how it usually runs in circles. Soon the coin will be swinging in circles. Switch to thinking "deer" and the coin will go back to moving in a straight line. Let the other player hold the string, just to prove that the one holding it is not making the coin change directions.

Bean Guess

Place a number of beans in a jar. Count before and place a piece of paper with the number of beans written on it inside the jar. Set the jar on a table with a pencil, several slips of paper and a box to put the slips in. Each person guesses how many beans are in the jar, writes a number on a slip of paper with his name, and places it in the box. Sometime during the party, check the slips to see who came closest to the correct number and award a prize.

Brain Teaser

Write the following on a blackboard, a sheet of poster paper, a large sheet of paper or individual pieces of paper for each player: A _____ old woman on _____ bent, picked up her _____ and said "Come, _____, son, let us see whom we can _____ off today." Each word has the same letters arranged to spell different words. Have the participants show the words that they think are right to the leader secretly so that the others can continue to work on the problem. Do not tell the answers to the players if you are going to have them for a party again. Let them keep working on it. (Answer: vile, evil, veil, Levi, live)

Just One Word

On squares of cardboard or large sheets of paper or index cards, write the letters J U S T O N E W O R D. Mix them up on top of a table or on the floor or on a bed. Tell the players to make "just one word" out of the letters. If there are enough players, divide them into teams and have them racing against each other.

Sign In Mural

Tape a large sheet of white shelf paper or poster paper on the wall or on a table near the door where people are entering the room for a party. Crayons, Magic Markers, or tempera paint and brushes should be close by. As each person enters the room, ask him to "sign in" by drawing something on the paper and signing his name. Leave it on the wall for a decoration and "conversation piece" for the party.

Decorators' Relay

Divide the room into four parts with a table in each section. Place on the table crepe paper, balloons, posters, tape, and anything which can be used for decorations. Divide the people into four teams and assign them each a corner. On the signal, the team members start decorating their corner of the room. Give a time limit of five or ten minutes. Vote to determine who did the best job. At the end of the party, have another contest to see which team can take down the decorations and clean up their corner the quickest.

Match and Fix

Before the party, prepare a number of tickets. If it is a special holiday, make them in appropriate shapes like stars, shamrocks, Valentines, firecrackers, pumpkins or use different colors of paper. Cut each in half with a jigsaw edge. After a few people have arrived at the party, give them half of a ticket and ask them to move around the room to find the person with the other half. The two people will be partners for the next game.

Who's Got My Bone

A group game requiring little space and physical activity for any number of players, probably children. The bone may be an eraser or similar flat object. The players' chairs are placed in a row or rows behind the "doggy's" chair, which is a few feet away from the rest. One player is chosen to be the "doggy." The doggy is asked to cover his eyes or he is blindfolded. Then the leader chooses someone to steal the doggy's bone. The bone is hidden under the player or in his clothes so it cannot be seen by the doggy when he turns around. Leader says "OK" when the bone is out of sight and the doggy gets three guesses to find his bone. The player caught with the bone becomes the new doggy.

Chair Leg Toss

Turn a chair upside down so that its legs are sticking out toward players at right angles. Mark off a throwing line. Each player gets four rings (jar rubbers, embroidery hoops, quoits) and tries to make a ringer over each chair leg. Establish a scoring system such as one point for each ringer. Player who gets ten points first wins.

Animal Noise

In small envelopes place a card (or valentine) which is pinned on the patient as he enters the room. Each one opens the envelope (one at a time) and finds the name of an animal or other noise making object on the card. He must then make the noise of the animal. To the tune of "My Bonnie" they make the noise of their animals all together. What a noise! This is good for relaxing the group and getting them in the mood for having fun.

Package Mixer

Wrap packages with large hearts on the outside (for Valentine Party) with funny contents, like a woman's garter, bobby pin, pair of suspenders, beer can opener, toothpick, and other gifts. While music plays, pass the package from one person to another around the circle. When the music stops, that person who is holding the package opens it. After the laughter dies down, start another package around, skipping the person who got the last one. After each has a package, let them swap around if they want a different gift. This game is a good mixer.

Balloon Therapy

Blow up a balloon and tie it to the bed of a CVA patient or others who may have little use of hands. Let them bat the balloon around to see how long they can keep it in the air. If there are several patients in the room, let them bat it from one bed to another.

I Know Club

Players are seated in a circle or anywhere in a room. The

leader announces that he wants some new members for the "I Know Club." The object of the game is for the players to spot the clue, which is the vowel *i*. If a player names any word containing the vowel *i*, he is refused membership, but not told why. He may know books, but not magazines, pals but not friends; fowl but not chicken. Do not give the secret away for this game can go on for weeks in a group which meets frequently.

Descriptive Initials

Players are seated in a circle, or around tables, or in little groups, or lying in beds in a ward. Starting with one player, each introduces the person on his right by using adjectives starting with his initials. If the person's name is Francis Clark, he might be introduced as "Francis Clark, who is fantastically clever." If the players are well acquainted they can also use slams as well as compliments.

Detective

One patient or player is selected to be "it" and that person is turned around in front of the other players to be carefully observed. The person is then taken from the room and changes something about his appearance, such as putting his watch on the other wrist, or changing a pin from one side of a dress to the other. When the person is brought back into the room, the other players must discover what it is that is different. The player who guesses correctly first gets a prize.

Shouting Proverbs

The players form two or more teams and each team chooses a familiar proverb, such as "All that glitters is not gold." Each member on the team is assigned one word of the proverb, with the same word being given to more than one person if necessary. Each team chooses a leader, who gives the count of three for a starting signal. On the fourth downbeat of the hand, all shout in unison the word which each has been assigned. The other teams try to guess what the proverb is. They may gather around the outside of the shouting group and listen for one word for a clue. The first team to guess the proverb is the next team to do the shouting. If the proverb is not guessed after four or five trys, let the team tell what their proverb is. Do not drag the game out.

Hunter, Fox or Gun

This game may be played with two persons or many. If more than two, divide the players into teams and place them at opposite sides of the room, where they sit or stand facing. Each team has a leader who decides whether his team will be the hunter, fox or gun. He then goes down the line whispering what it is to each person. They must be all the same. On the signal, both teams do the action for their word. The "fox" sticks thumbs in ears and waggles fingers. The "gun" is one finger on one hand pointing with "Bang!" The "hunter" stands with hands on hips. Score as follows: The hunter scores over the gun, because he can shoot it; the gun scores over the rabbit, because it can kill it; and the rabbit scores over the hunter because he can outrun it. Play for ten points.

Magazine Scavenger Hunt

Make a list of several articles and give each player a list and a magazine to find the pictures in. The articles on the list are torn out of the magazine, such as a picture of a black and white dog, or an ad for Campbell's soup, or a picture of a train.

Alphabet Scavenger Hunt

Divide the players into groups and sit them as far apart as possible from the other groups. On the signal, each group tries to find as many articles as possible starting with each letter of the alphabet. They could have an ashtray for *A*, a bracelet for *B*, and so on. The articles must be found in the room or within each group. At the end of ten minutes or so, stop the hunt and have each team tell you what they have for each letter of the alphabet. The other teams may challenge anything which they think fails to qualify, such as crossing two pencils and calling it an article for X. The team which has the most articles for the alphabet wins. The leader will find that the last group to go through its articles will have added quite a few while getting ideas from preceding teams!

Alphabet Cards

Make a set of alphabet cards, with large letters printed on sheets of cardboard. Shuffle them and place them face up. Choose a category like birds, animals, fruit, flowers, trees and others. As each card is picked up and shown, the players try to give a word in that category that starts with that letter. The first person to give the word gets the card. If nobody gives a word within five or ten seconds, put the card back on the bottom of the deck. The person who gets the most cards wins the game.

Word Toss

Instead of using small dice with letters, cut larger ones from imitation styrofoam, about one inch square, and put letters on with a black Magic Marker. About fourteen cubes are needed.

Cover All

To play the game, you need two large dice, a round shaker which can be made by cutting a Dermasage bottle in half and putting Kleenex on the bottom to absorb the noise, and strips of paper 2 inches wide and 11 inches long marked from 2 to 12. Each player has a strip of paper. Shake the dice and cover with a bingo chip the number which comes up. Keep shaking and throwing dice until the player gets a number which is already covered. He then passes the dice on to the next player. The player who gets all of the numbers covered first wins the game.

People Bingo

Make bingo cards on 8½ x 11 sheets of paper. As people enter the room for a party, ask them to get autographs, one name in each square. When all of the people have arrived, ask them to sit down with their bingo cards and a pencil. One person reads the name of another person and all cross that name out on their cards. Then the person whose name was called gives the name of someone else, and that name is crossed out. When someone has five names crossed out, as in bingo, he is the winner. Play the game until several have won. This is a good game for getting acquainted.

Another version of People Bingo is to write B I N G O across the top of the card, as on a bingo card. Then go from person to person and fill in the squares with the following key, which should be written on the side of the card:

B—a first name; I—where from; N—color of eyes; G—name of someone wearing pink or blue; O—name of someone wearing a watch or bracelet. The first two people to get bingo win prizes.

SOME GAMES WHICH HAVE BEEN PLAYED WITH RETARDED CHILDREN

Balance Relay

The first child in each line has a book or flat surface object. He puts it on his head, keeping it balanced. He walks to a prescribed area and back. This continues until all have had a turn. The first line to finish wins the race.

Balloon Volley Ball

This game is played like regular volley ball. Do not expect them to hit it back. Most of the time they will catch it and throw it back. But this still gives them a lot of fun.

Bottle Bowling

Set up a number of plastic bottles and have the children knock them down with a playground ball.

Dodge Ball

Students form a circle. One who is it stands in the center. The others have a playground ball or a balloon. All try to hit the student in the middle of the circle. The one who hits him then goes into the center. They should be told to throw to hit below the knees.

Drop the Ball

Have the students form a circle. Have one student with

a ball go around and drop the ball behind another person. He picks up the ball and chases the dropper of the ball, trying to tag him before he gets back to the position that was left open. If he fails to tag him he goes around and drops the ball behind someone else. The same pattern should continue until everyone has had at least one turn.

Hand Ball

First child in each line has a ball. On command from the leader he runs to a prescribed point and back again giving the ball to the next in line. This continues until all have had a turn. The first line to finish wins.

Head Ball Relay

First child in each line is given a ball and told to push it with his head to a prescribed point and back again to the start. Continue on down the line.

Marching

Marching is a very good activity for the retarded. This activity can be incorporated in a rhythm band, which you will find most children like. You can make all of the instruments from material directly on hand.

Rattle: Plastic bottle containing marbles or pebbles.
Rhythm sticks: Two round sticks.
Bottle drum: Plastic bottle and a stick.
Pie drum: A tin pie plate and old spoon.
Cappets: Bottle caps nailed loosely on a stick.
Spoon: Hit two spoons together.

Musical Chairs

Make a circle of chairs. Have the children march around to music. Make sure you have one less chair than students. Stop the music. Have them sit down quickly. Those not having a seat must sit on the sidelines. The last one to get a seat is the winner, but with the retarded, winning is unimportant. This game can also be played with benches by placing pages from a catalog along the bench and not letting them sit where the papers are.

Sailor Over the Water

The children form a circle holding hands. One person in the center is "It." The children march around him repeating this verse:

> Sailor over the water, sailor over the sea,
> Sailor can catch a fish, but sailor can't catch me,

On the word "me," everybody squats down. The person who is "It" tries to tag someone before they squat down. Then the one tagged goes in the circle.

Train Game

Have the students march around in a circle pretending that they are the cars on a train. The leader should have a whistle. At different intervals he blows the whistle and all the children squat quickly on the floor. You can start off walking very slowly then speed up. They may also skip along. This game gives children a lot of fun and a lot of good exercise.

Rope Exercises

Tie the two ends of a rope to make a circle. Each child finds a space on the rope equal distance from the others. They tighten the rope to make a circle. Holding their feet in place, they lean back with arms straight. On the command to run back, everyone pulls straight backward. Be sure they pull back evenly. Have them turn around and do the same thing in this position. This time they pull forward steadily. Have them put both hands on the rope and run in a circle, being sure to pull on the rope at the same time. Stop and reverse directions. Have them put the rope over their heads and down to the ground, being sure to vary the pace. Have them lay on their stomachs holding the rope with arms straight and do back lifts, raising up off their chests and holding the rope stiff armed.

A variation of this is the Snail Walk. Holding the rope,

children put hands up and over the shoulder behind, bend over at the waist, walk slowly. Maybe they can learn the Snail Walk poem.

> Snail, snail, creep in your shell,
> Snail, snail, follow well.
> Wind, wind, keep in line,
> Follow the leader, keep in line.

Medicine Ball Tag

Play normal tag, but "It" carries the medicine ball. He tags and soon as the child is tagged, the new "It" takes the ball and becomes "It."

Plastic Bottle Obstacle Course

All in the group have a plastic bottle. Have them place it in front of them, between their big toes. The group runs around the outside of the bottles. At the whistle, all go and stand in front of the bottle, or players go in and out without touching any bottles and at the whistle they find their own.

Back to Back Relay

Form two lines, back to back. On command, both lines run in the direction in which they are facing. At the whistle, they run back to the starting line, get back to back with partner and sit down.

PENCIL AND PAPER FUN

People who are confined to wheelchairs or beds can have fun with pencil and paper games, or quizzes. This gives them mental exercise and an opportunity to compete with others in passive pastimes.

Here are a few games for your use. Watch for others in magazines, books and on television.

Musical Wedding

Fill in with song titles: It was a very _____ when _____ and _____ were married while the _____ was played by _____. They were married at _____, and were attended by

_____ and _____. On their honeymoon they sailed down _____ and saw _____ and after following _____ they crossed _____ and finally reached _____. After a happy month they _____. They were met by _____ who drove them across the hills to their _____ where they had their first quarrel because he left her _____ in the _____ while he and _____ were down on the corner singing _____. Then _____ went back to _____ and _____ said "I suppose _____" but he wired "_____" and she replied "_____ and meet your _____ in _____." He met her _____, they started back to their own _____ and from that time on life for them was one _____ after another. Each Sunday they went to _____ and even after Father Time had sprinkled _____ their romance was just a continuation of _____.

The Match Game

This game is good for persons eight to fourteen years of age, but could be played with any age. Materials needed are paper, pencils and play money or some other score keeping device. The leader sits to one side and players sit on beds if hospitalized, or around small tables in a play area. The leader makes up short sentences leaving a blank at the end. She chooses how the sentence will be completed and writes her answer on her paper. The players complete each statement as they think the leader will. They have a specified time to complete the statements. When the time is up, each player gives his answer. The players who match the leader get points or play money. For example, the leader may write "Mary fell down and broke her _____." She may fill in the statement with "leg." Players 1 and 2 may also complete the sentence with "leg" and players 3, 4 and 5 with "arm." Players 1 and 2 will collect points or play money because they have matched the leader's choice of a fill in.

Draw a House

Give all players a sheet of paper and a small pencil or crayon. The players close their eyes and are told by the leader to draw the frame of a house, sun in the sky, chimney on the roof, sidewalk in front of the house, clouds in the sky, flowers in front of the house, a television antenna on the roof, windows in the house, a ball on the front lawn, and a door in the house.

Have the players open their eyes and look at their drawings. Much laughter and conversation will follow about the master-pieces. If any players are blind, have someone who is sighted describe their pictures to them.

Mobile Quiz Cart

Use picture quizzes, fill-in-the-blank quizzes, or others that can be mounted on cardboard. Tape them to all four sides of a hospital cart and wheel them from one ward to another where they can be "parked" for a time while the patients work on them. Then wheel them to another area.

Fun Folios

Have volunteers assemble Fun Folios, including quizzes, riddles, crossword puzzles, directions for solitaire games, jokes and other fun for one. These can be distributed to patients throughout the hospital or institution.

Modern Art Illustrations

Find or draw pictures of a mirror, sponge, sixteen cubes of sugar on a saucer, an umbrella, scissors, clothesline, thumb tacks on tea bags, two unlighted candles, a pair of dice and a piece of wood with a nail in it. Give the players the pictures and the following list of picture titles. Opposite the title, they should list the number of the picture which they think best fits it.

Titles: Out for the Night; The Reigning Favorite; A Line From Home; A Place for Reflection; Sweet Sixteen; Paradise; An Absorbing Subject; Little Peace Maker; Revolutionary Act; Drive Through the Vienna Wood.

Stock Exchange

Each player is given a chart with 25 squares drawn on it, five down and five across. The players take turns calling out a letter of the alphabet. As a letter is called, everyone puts it down in any one of the squares. The next player then calls out a letter which may or may not have been given before. The game continues until 25 letters have been called and all squares filled.

The aim of each player is to arrange the letters so that words are formed both in the horizontal and vertical rows. Of course it will hardly ever be possible to use all of the letters in words since a letter may not be moved once it has been written down. Proper names and words of less than three letters are not credited. A word of five letters counts five points, four letters count three points and three letters count one point. Both horizontal and vertical rows are counted but short words within the longer ones do not count.

Observation Quiz

Have you noticed any of the following:
1. What four words appear besides "In God We Trust" on almost all U.S. coins?
2. What colors other than white appear on the dollar bill?
3. Does Lincoln wear a tie?
4. How wide would you say a penny is?
5. Identify the building on the back of a Jefferson nickel.
6. What seven letter word other than *America* appears on all U.S. Currency of less than a dollar.
7. What letter does not appear on your phone dial, nor does it appear in the name of any of our states.
8. If you are a man, give the total number of lace holes in your shoes.
9. What time do clock advertisements usually show?
10. A fork has how many tines?
11. Which way does the knob of a door turn when opening?
12. When water goes down a drain does it go clockwise or counterclockwise?

Musical Occupations

Players have sheets of paper numbered to 14 and pencils. Someone plays the songs on the piano or a record player or an accordian, and players write down the occupation indicated in the song.

1. Dancer—"After the Ball" or "The Band Played On"
2. Jeweler—"Ring around the Rosie"
3. Gardener—"White Coral Bells"
4. Boatman—"Volga Boatman"
5. Rancher or Cowboy—"Home on the Range"
6. Snowplow operator—"White Christmas"
7. Taxi driver—"Dark Town Strutter's Ball"
8. Engineer or conductor—"I've Been Working on the Railroad"
9. Milliner—"Easter Bonnet"
10. Miner—"Clementine"
11. Shepherd—"The First Noel"
12. Teacher—"School Days"
13. Miller—"Down By the Old Mill Stream"
14. Pilot—"Air Force Song"

SIMPLE DRAMATICS

One does not need a cast of professionals and a three act play for a program in Dramatics. There are many quickies that can be done at a minute's notice and in about that much time. Everybody has some "ham" in him and everybody can get into the act in the following ideas for dramatics.

Rapid Fire Actors

Players are divided into groups and each group has a leader or actor. On a signal, the captain runs up to the leader who gives the name of a book, movie, television show, or other category. He must announce before the game which category it is. As soon as the captains get the title, they run back to the group and act out in pantomime something to give the group a clue as to what it is. As soon as the group guesses, all actors run to the leader and get another title.

Pantomimes

Pass out slips of paper with assignments for pantomimes. Go around the circle and let each person do his pantomime and have the other players guess what it is. Some ideas for pantomiming:

1. Threading a needle.
2. Arranging flowers in a vase.
3. Shoveling snow.
4. Tuning the radio for a favorite program.
5. Crossing a brook on stepping stones.
6. Hanging out the laundry.
7. Playing solitaire.
8. Fishing.
9. Modeling in clay.
10. Crossing a busy street.

Think up some others!

Paper Bag Dramatics

Fill some shopping bags with about six articles, such as a doll, a piece of bubble gum, a paper plate, an old shirt, an old candle and a balloon. Divide the players into groups. Give each group a bag of props and tell them to plan a little skit using all of the props. They can have about ten minutes to prepare the skit. Then let each group present their skit for the entertainment of the others.

Guess a Skit

Divide players into groups of five or six players. Assign each group a type of skit which they will do. One group may act out a newspaper headline that all would have heard or read. Another group might act out a nursery rhyme; another a song title; another a historical event and so on. Give them five or ten minutes to work up the skit. Each group presents the skit and when they have finished, the other players try to guess what they were acting out.

Chapter 9

FUN AIDS

Tips for recreation programs are everywhere if you keep your eyes and ears open. One of the best sources for ideas is people. The people whom you are recreating, fellow recreation leaders, books and magazines, publications and mass media are giving leads, if you will listen and read.

There are many sources for free films, free materials for craft projects, free entertainment and free fun for the asking. The following are some sources that you should explore:

Schools and colleges   Dance clubs
Local organizations   Local merchants
Veterans' organizations   Factories
Churches   Local newspapers
Libraries   Rummage sales

Here are other ideas contributed by some recreation leaders:

Supermarket chains will often supply letters of credit for their local outlets if one writes to the central office and requests particular items for a specific event.

Family Circle and *Woman's Day* have good ideas. World Wide Games, Delaware, Ohio, sell many good games. Write for their catalog.

Good Old Days magazine, *Ideals* magazine, *Pack-O-Fun* and American Felt Company are good resources.

American Dance Therapy Association and correspondence with persons belonging to it, and the Sacred Dance Guild are good sources to explore.

Here are some "inspiration joggers" for programs which could be provided by the recreation staff, the people who are being entertained, volunteers or organizations in the community:

Barbershop quartets, Sweet Adelines   Choral reading
Church choirs   Rhythm band

Minstrel shows
Sing-a-longs
Tea parties
Family dinners
  (invite the families of patients in)
Hymn sings
Bus or automobile rides
Gardening
Fashion shows (serious or funny)
Church services
Bookcarts and games carts
Tournaments (bowling, pingpong,
  horseshoes, *anything*)
Game night (table games)
Lectures
Slide shows
Home movies
Discussion groups
"Great Decisions" discussions
Play reading

Kitchen band
Dances
Nature walks
Picnics
Bird watching (feeders outside
  windows)
Charm courses
Poetry reading
Painting, sculpturing, and other arts
  and crafts classes
Flower arranging demonstrations
Puppet shows
Concerts
Folk singers
Card playing
Bingo
Coffee hours
Service projects
Cooking classes
Camera clubs

SOME HELPFUL PUBLICATIONS

The Complete Book of Children's Play, Ruth Hartly, Robert Goldenson, Thomas Y. Crowell Company, New York, 1957.

Recreation Leadership, H. Dan Corbin. Prentice-Hall, Inc. New York, 1953.

Complete Book of Games and Stunts, Darwin A. Hindman. Prentice-Hall, Inc., New Jersey, 1956.

Red is the Color of Hurting, Planning for Children in the Hospital, U.S. Department of Health, Education and Welfare.

All in Play, Rowena M. Shoemaker, Play Schools Association, Inc., 41 West 57th St., New York.

Play in a Hospital, Play Schools Association.

On the Mend (recreation in hospitals), International Recreation Association, 345 East 46th St., New York.

Recreation, A Medical Viewpoint, Paul Haun. Bureau of Publications, Teachers College, Columbia University, New York, 1965.

Recreation in Treatment Centers, published annually by the National

Therapeutic Society. Available from National Recreation and Park Association, 1700 Pennsylvania Avenue, N.W., Washington, D.C. 20006.

Therapeutic Recreation Journal, published quarterly by the National Therapeutic Recreation Society. Available with membership in the Society.

Play Activities for the Retarded Child, Bernice W. Carlson, David Grigland.

Good Old Days magazine, Tower Press, Inc., P.O. Box 412, Danvers, Mass. $4 per year for subscription.

Handbook for Volunteers in Mental Hospitals, University of Minnesota Press.

Experiencing the Patient's Day, Ida J. Davies.

Recreation for the Physically Handicapped, Janet Pomeroy.

Activities for the Aged and Infirm, Toni Merrill. Thomas, Springfield, 1967.

Crafts for the Elderly, Elaine and Loren Gould. Thomas, Springfield, 1971.

Handcrafts for the Homebound Handicapped, Mildred Kroll Rich, Thomas, Springfield, 1960.

A Guide to Books On Recreation. Publications Center, National Recreation and Park Association, 1700 Pennsylvania Avenue, NW, Washington, D.C. 20006.

Chapter 10

FUN IN THE COMMUNITY

Once upon a time, not too long ago really, when a person entered an institution for the mentally ill or retarded, or a home for the aging, nursing home or other agency for the care of the aging or handicapped, he entered another small world. He may have been cut off from the community, family ties and all knowledge of the outside world.

This situation is rapidly changing and many leaders of recreation in these settings can take much credit for effecting this change. For they are the people who are taking the patients back into the community, or bringing volunteers from the community into the agency. Through bus rides, visits to parks and other places of interest, shopping trips, attendance at movies, concerts and other community entertainments, patients are becoming reoriented to the world outside. If they have recently become residents in the institution, they will not lose touch with the community because of these activities.

Volunteers who visit the institutions to bring in entertainment for the patients also bring a tie with the outside world.

There is a "bridging of the gap" between institution and community, especially in recreation, which is most heartening. Interaction among community and institution recreation leaders can provide a wider range of recreational opportunities for the patients. Facilities for recreation in institution and community can be shared.

Look around *your* community and see how you can use the available resources for providing fun for your patients. Preceding chapters have given a few ideas for resources.

One community is sharing its resources this way:

Our major goal is to expand and enhance the human resources of our people and the natural resources of our land by bringing the two increasingly together. We believe that the free and creative

83

use of leisure time, in activity or contemplation, is fundamental to the vitality and joy of human life and we believe that the finest recreation programs are needed to help bring the value to every life. More so with the handicapped and the mentally retarded who are at a loss for time.

Henceforth, we are trying to promote and to develop good, clean, wholesome recreation for the handicapped and retarded in this area.

Local community recreation centers have already done much for this program, with special events scheduled for the retarded such as Halloween parties, Christmas parties and special monthly dances. The community recreation department is also working in conjunction with the local schools in a recreation program of swimming and bowling weekly for retarded children. Preschool tap and ballet classes are available one afternoon a week at the Community House.

A neighboring community's contribution to this program rates high with many loyal volunteers as promoters and workers. Music classes are held at the American Legion Hall, as well as a monthly record hop. The Junior Chamber of Commerce sponsored the Junior Olympics this year for the retarded. The Children's Christmas Party last year was sponsored by the Lawyers' Bar Association.

We have everyone and everything going for us and this certainly will help us reach our goal in providing fun for the retarded.

One hospital is taking advantage of community resources this way:

The main concern of the Leisure Education Program is to provide the patient returning to the community with enriched leisure skills. Throughout the past year, the department has utilized staff, patients and outside community agencies to assist in providing pathways to these goals. Attempts have been made to reach into every facet of recreation existing in the community. This is important in order that the patient might leave with some basic background in leisure endeavors which are available to him or her.

The program this year has included demonstrations, exhibitions, activities sponsored by the National Association of Professional Gardeners, Tandy Leather Corporation, Cortland Fishing Line Company, Eastman Kodak, Revlon Cosmetics, Singer Sewing Machine Corporation, Somerset County Parks and Recreation Commission, Edison Recreation Commission and Somerset County Library, among others. Consequently, not only do our patients directly benefit from the program, but also the Clinic receives added note and public relation throughout the community.